TOP 100 ROCK

BANDS, ACTS, ARTISTS

D1494498

Publisher and Creative Director: Nick Wells
Project Editor: Sara Robson
Art Director: Mike Spender
Layout Design: Jane Ashley
Digital Design and Production: Chris Herbert

Special thanks to: Helen Crust, Chelsea Edwards, Victoria Garrard, Anna Groves, Geoffrey Meadon,
Polly Prior, Digby Smith and Catherine Taylor

First published 2010 by
FLAME TREE PUBLISHING
Crabtree Hall, Crabtree Lane
Fulham, London SW6 6TY
United Kingdom

www.flametreepublishing.com

Music information site: www.flametreemusic.com

10 12 14 13 11

1 3 5 7 9 10 8 6 4 2

Flame Tree is part of The Foundry Creative Media Company Ltd

The CIP record for this book is available from the British Library.

ISBN: 978-1-84786-966-1

Printed in China

TOP 100 ROCK
BANDS, ACTS, ARTISTS

RICHARD BUSKIN, ALAN CLAYSON, JOE CUSHLEY, RUSTY CUTCHIN, HUGH FIELDER,
MIKE GENT, JAKE KENNEDY, COLIN SALTER, IAN SHIRLEY AND JOHN TOBLER

GENERAL EDITOR: MICHAEL HEATLEY
FOREWORD BY ED POTTON

**FLAME TREE
PUBLISHING**

CONTENTS

Publisher's Note 8

Foreword 12

Introduction 17

ABBA 26

AC/DC 30

Aerosmith 32

The Allman Brothers Band 34

The Animals 38

The Band 40

The Beach Boys 42

The Beatles 48

The Bee Gees 54

Chuck Berry 56

Black Sabbath 62

Blur 66

Bon Jovi 68

David Bowie 70

James Brown 76

The Byrds 82

Johnny Cash 84

Chicago 86

Eric Clapton 88

The Clash 90

Coldplay 94

Sam Cooke 96

Elvis Costello 98

Cream 100

Creedence Clearwater Revival . . . 102

Crosby, Stills & Nash 104

Def Leppard 106

Bo Diddley 108

Dire Straits 110

The Doors 112

Bob Dylan 116

The Eagles 122

Eminem 126

Fleetwood Mac 128

Foo Fighters 132

Aretha Franklin 134

Marvin Gaye 140

Genesis 146

The Grateful Dead 150

Green Day 154

Guns N'Roses 156

Bill Haley 158

Jimi Hendrix 160

Buddy Holly 166

Howlin' Wolf 168

Iron Maiden 170

Michael Jackson 172

Jethro Tull 176

Elton John 178

Janis Joplin 182

Muddy Waters 226

Nirvana 228

Oasis 234

Parliament-Funkadelic 236

Pearl Jam 238

Tom Petty 240

Pink Floyd 242

The Police 248

Elvis Presley 252

Prince 258

Queen 262

Radiohead 268

B.B. King 184

The Kinks 188

Led Zeppelin 190

Jerry Lee Lewis 196

Little Richard 200

Lynyrd Skynyrd 206

Madonna 208

Bob Marley 212

Metallica 218

Joni Mitchell 220

The Moody Blues 222

Van Morrison 224

The Ramones 270

Red Hot Chili Peppers 272

R.E.M. 274

Smokey Robinson
   & The Miracles 276

The Rolling Stones 278

Roxy Music 284

Santana 286

The Sex Pistols 290

Simon & Garfunkel 292

Sly & The Family Stone 294

Bruce Springsteen
   & The E Street Band 296

Status Quo 302

Rod Stewart 304

T. Rex 306

Tina Turner 308

U2 310

Van Halen 314

The Velvet Underground 318

The White Stripes 320

The Who 322

Stevie Wonder 328

The Yardbirds 334

Yes 336

Neil Young 338

Frank Zappa 342

ZZ Top 344

Acknowledgements 346

Further Reading 348

Index 350

PUBLISHER'S NOTE

When we were deciding who should be included in this book, two main questions arose. First, and perhaps the most obvious, is what exactly do we mean by 'rock' music? And second, what qualifies an artist (bands and soloists, just to clarify) to be deemed the 'best-ever'? So before we get down to the nitty gritty of who is in, who is out and who nearly made it, perhaps we first need to (try to) tackle the thorny issues raised here.

WHAT IS ROCK MUSIC?

Strictly speaking, 'rock' music is the genre that emerged in the 1950s out of a heady mixture of rock'n'roll, rhythm and blues and country, with perhaps a little folk, jazz, gospel and classical thrown in for good measure. Like anything, it has been altered over the subsequent decades by myriad social, cultural, technological and political influences, all of which have informed and shaped it. And because it is the familiar language of youth, every generation has taken it, shaken it and made it their own. So we decided that for the purposes of this book, when we refer to 'rock' music we are not talking simply about the sound made by a four–piece band consisting of a lead singer, two guitarists and a drummer, but are using it as an all–encompassing term to draw in blues, pop, soul, funk, punk, rockabilly, heavy metal, reggae, garage and rap as well.

WHO QUALIFIES?

To be in *Top 100 Rock* you have to be pretty darn good. That goes without saying, but what is the magic ingredient that our candidates need to have to warrant their selection? Is it purely based on their music? What their lyrics have to say to us? Is it their merits as performers, how well they strut their groovy stuff? Or is it something else, something you can't quite put your finger on? In the end, we settled on the idea that it was a blend of all these elements, and that the artists' music should, in some way, have etched a mark in popular culture.

THE SELECTION

So, now to the selection. We won't go through the reasons behind the choice of each artist as we don't have the space, but will say that to single out those who have contributed something to the greater good of rock'n'roll is quite a process. We came up with categories so it was easier to make our picks. Here they are, with a few examples from each one.

1. There are those who were there at the beginning, without whom none of the rest of them would be there: Howlin' Wolf, Sam Cooke, Chuck Berry, B.B. King, Elvis Presley and Smokey Robinson.
2. There are those who came along next, added to what had been done before and created something entirely new – some are still going: The Beatles, The Beach Boys, Cream, The Rolling Stones, Bob Dylan, Jimi Hendrix and Sly & The Family Stone.
3. There are the ones who took things to a whole new level and never looked back: Aerosmith, Bon Jovi, Iron Maiden, Led Zeppelin and Queen.

4. There are those who went off in an entirely new direction, paving the way for those to come: The Grateful Dead, Eminem, The Ramones, The Sex Pistols, The Who and Frank Zappa.

5. Other candidates are just great at what they do, many who continue to be so, and who are regarded with great reverence: ABBA, Aretha Franklin, Michael Jackson, Madonna, Bob Marley and Stevie Wonder.

6. Finally, there are those who have inherited the mantle and in turn are influencing those who will be included in future editions of this book: Coldplay, Green Day, Nirvana, R.E.M., U2 and The White Stripes.

OUR PICK OF THE PICKS

As if choosing 100 of the best-ever-artists was not enough, we decided that to really stir things up, we would categorize our picks in a 1–100 list, so as to come up with who (in our opinion) is the rightful wearer of the best-ever-artist crown. This list, shown on the opposite page, it should be remembered, is purely subjective and has been devised as a means of provoking debate. As a source of further provocation, we have asked Ed Potton, who has kindly written our Foreword, to come up with his 1–100 choices (see page 15). If you would like to give us your opinion, tell us who we have missed out, give us your 1–100 list or generally agree/rant with what you have read, then we'd love to hear from you. You can contact us in the usual ways, or get in touch via the Flame Tree Music page on Facebook.

Flame Tree Publishing, 2010

OUR TOP 100

1. The Beatles
2. Elvis Presley
3. Led Zeppelin
4. Nirvana
5. Chuck Berry
6. Jimi Hendrix
7. Bob Dylan
8. The Rolling Stones
9. James Brown
10. The Who
11. Stevie Wonder
12. Little Richard
13. Pink Floyd
14. The Beach Boys
15. Aretha Franklin
16. Marvin Gaye
17. Queen
18. David Bowie
19. Bob Marley
20. Bruce Springsteen
    & The E Street Band
21. U2
22. The Doors
23. Black Sabbath
24. Elton John
25. Neil Young
26. Jerry Lee Lewis
27. B.B. King
28. Prince
29. Van Halen
30. The Grateful Dead
31. The Clash
32. Michael Jackson
33. Madonna

34. The Eagles
35. Fleetwood Mac
36. The Allman Brothers Band
37. The Police
38. Santana
39. Genesis
40. ABBA
41. Buddy Holly
42. Sam Cooke
43. Bo Diddley
44. Sly & The Family Stone
45. The Velvet Underground
46. The Kinks
47. Elvis Costello
48. Cream
49. Crosby, Stills & Nash
50. Parliament–Funkadelic
51. Frank Zappa
52. The Ramones
53. Simon & Garfunkel
54. Janis Joplin
55. Eric Clapton
56. AC/DC
57. The Byrds
58. Van Morrison
59. Smokey Robinson
    & The Miracles
60. Johnny Cash
61. Joni Mitchell
62. Creedence Clearwater Revival
63. R.E.M.
64. Metallica
65. Aerosmith
66. Yes

67. Pearl Jam
68. The Band
69. The Sex Pistols
70. Bill Haley
71. The Bee Gees
72. Guns N'Roses
73. Tom Petty
74. Radiohead
75. The Yardbirds
76. The Moody Blues
77. Chicago
78. ZZ Top
79. Dire Straits
80. Red Hot Chili Peppers
81. Bon Jovi
82. Jethro Tull
83. Lynyrd Skynyrd
84. The Animals
85. Iron Maiden
86. Coldplay
87. Muddy Waters
88. Howlin' Wolf
89. Rod Stewart
90. Tina Turner
91. Eminem
92. Roxy Music
93. T. Rex
94. Def Leppard
95. Status Quo
96. Green Day
97. The White Stripes
98. Foo Fighters
99. Oasis
100. Blur

FOREWORD

What's the greatest rock act of all time? It's a question that has long occupied bar-room jousters, rampant list obsessives and slackers with too much time on their hands. It's a question, of course, that generally produces one of two answers – Elvis or The Beatles – more of which later. But how about the Top 100 rock acts of all time? That should occupy you for a fair bit longer. The following pages offer some persuasive suggestions. You won't agree with them all, of course. That would be dull, not to say obsequious. As ever with lists, healthy disagreement is integral to the exercise.

So, what do you need to know about this Top 100? Well, the first thing to say is that – other than a Jamaican (Bob Marley), four Irishmen (U2), some Canadians (The Band), a set of Aussies (AC/DC) and quartet of tuneful Swedes (ABBA) – it's composed of American and British acts. This is unsurprising: English is the language of rock'n'roll, and the US and the UK are blessed with dynamic music industries and cosmopolitan musical hubs that the other anglophone countries lack: London and New York, Liverpool and Chicago, Glasgow and Detroit.

These two musical superpowers seem to excel at different things, however. Of our Top 100, more than a quarter are US solo artists, against just four from the UK. The numbers are more or less equal when it comes to groups, although – by my reckoning at least (see below) – seven of the top 10 bands are British. Does this reflect a contrast between American individualism and British collaboration?

Perhaps. Does it suggest that Yanks are more natural show-offs, while Limeys like safety in numbers? Probably.

But how do we judge these titans against each other? Comparison, though undeniably fun, is akin to stacking bubbles, especially when you're comparing artists who work in different genres. Because, as far as this book is concerned, rock doesn't just mean rock, it also means soul, funk, blues, hip-hop, folk and prog. I've put Eminem, for example, above Yes, but can you really compare a hyper-speed Slim Shady rhyme with a Rick Wakeman keyboard wig-out? I guess the question to be asked is whether the artist has transcended their genre – although in the case of hip-hop, Public Enemy, A Tribe Called Quest, the Wu-Tang Clan and Jay-Z all have at least as strong a case as Eminem.

Let me mark out my parameters. Versatile thoroughbreds (Stevie Wonder, David Bowie, Roxy Music – take a bow) trump powerful one-trick ponies (that's you at the back, Jimi Hendrix, Iron Maiden and Oasis). Those who write their own songs are generally preferred to those who sing other people's and, while pioneers certainly deserve credit, perfecters often deserve more. Hence the multi-instrumental cosmic-soul excursions of Stevie Wonder place him higher than the less ambitious but no less melodious ballads of Sam Cooke.

How to top the chart? Well, the winning act will need to have distinguished themselves in terms of impact, charisma, creativity, entertainment, depth, live performance, social relevance, originality, adventurousness and style over a period of years. They will also need to have left behind an unimpeachable legacy. It's a big ask. But hey, we're talking about the greatest musical act in the history of the world, not a two-bit talent show on Southend pier.

Based on these criteria, nine of my personal top 10 fall by the wayside. Queen, Dylan and ABBA were too rooted to their genres to be truly supreme. Wonder, Bowie, Jackson, Prince and The Stones, meanwhile, all endured later periods of relative underachievement – albums like *Characters*, *Tonight*, *Dangerous*, *Come* and *Dirty Work* aren't fit to lick the boots of *Innervisions*, *Low*, *Off The Wall*, *Sign 'O' The Times* and *Exile On Main St.* Longevity, sadly, is often a double-edged sword.

Of the aforementioned big two, Elvis would be many people's choice. But, though he reigns supreme in terms of performance, style and sheer, visceral impact, the King did not write enough of his own material to warrant the No. 1 spot – or even, in my opinion, 2 or 3.

Which leaves us with The Fab Four. Redefining rock and pop, foraying into folk, soul and psychedelia, excelling in the studio and on the stage, John, Paul, George and Ringo released at least half a dozen truly great albums and quit before they could soil their legacy with a bad one. Yes, predictable I know. But doesn't that predictability tell you something? Onward then, to my Top 100. Happy reading, and happy list making.

Ed Potton, 2010

MY TOP 100

1.	The Beatles	35.	B.B. King	67.	Def Leppard
2.	Stevie Wonder	36.	Bruce Springsteen	68.	Cream
3.	Michael Jackson		& The E Street Band	69.	Red Hot Chili Peppers
4.	Elvis Presley	37.	Buddy Holly	70.	Chicago
5.	David Bowie	38.	Chuck Berry	71.	Jerry Lee Lewis
6.	The Rolling Stones	39.	AC/DC	72.	The Doors
7.	Queen	40.	Sly & The Family Stone	73.	Metallica
8.	Prince	41.	U2	74.	ZZ Top
9.	ABBA	42.	Sam Cooke	75.	Muddy Waters
10.	Bob Dylan	43.	T. Rex	76.	Bill Haley
11.	Bob Marley	44.	R.E.M.	77.	Rod Stewart
12.	James Brown	45.	Coldplay	78.	Iron Maiden
13.	The Beach Boys	46.	Eminem	79.	The Yardbirds
14.	Madonna	47.	Elvis Costello	80.	The Animals
15.	Marvin Gaye	48.	Little Richard	81.	The Grateful Dead
16.	Roxy Music	49.	Frank Zappa	82.	Aerosmith
17.	Aretha Franklin	50.	Guns N'Roses	83.	The Band
18.	Led Zeppelin	51.	Fleetwood Mac	84.	Creedence Clearwater Revival
19.	Nirvana	52.	Blur	85.	Howlin' Wolf
20.	Neil Young	53.	Eric Clapton	86.	Green Day
21.	Radiohead	54.	Parliament-Funkadelic	87.	Crosby, Stills & Nash
22.	The Clash	55.	Oasis	88.	Foo Fighters
23.	The Bee Gees	56.	The Eagles	89.	Tom Petty
24.	Johnny Cash	57.	The Police	90.	The Allman Brothers Band
25.	Jimi Hendrix	58.	Smokey Robinson	91.	Bo Diddley
26.	The Velvet Underground		& The Miracles	92.	Jethro Tull
27.	Janis Joplin	59.	Simon & Garfunkel	93.	Santana
28.	The Sex Pistols	60.	Genesis	94.	Van Halen
29.	Joni Mitchell	61.	The Byrds	95.	The Moody Blues
30.	Van Morrison	62.	The White Stripes	96.	Lynyrd Skynyrd
31.	The Who	63.	Dire Straits	97.	Pearl Jam
32.	Pink Floyd	64.	Black Sabbath	98.	Tina Turner
33.	The Kinks	65.	Yes	99.	Bon Jovi
34.	Elton John	66.	The Ramones	100.	Status Quo

INTRODUCTION

As you will discover, it is harder than ever in the twenty-first century to place artists and their music in boxes or categories. When Run-DMC and Aerosmith brought rock and rap together back in 1986 their rock-rap fusion was considered unusual; since then, careers have been built on such cross-fertilization. Then there are figures like Madonna, constantly reinventing herself and moving from genre to genre. Samplers also mix and match by extracting musical phrases from well-known songs and building others around them, with the result that classics have enjoyed a new life and reached a new audience. All this makes the imposition of genres more difficult,

if not futile, hence the inclusion in this book of performers who may not be regarded as classic 'rock' artists. So, before exploring the artists identified in this book as the Top 100, it might be worth exploring the origins of rock music, and perhaps where it is heading in the new century.

The roots of rock music lie in black music. It was country and blues that came together in the 1950s to form Elvis Presley's brand of rock'n'roll, the spark that lit the fuse for the musical and cultural explosion that followed. This youth–orientated sound was the first to meld sexual energy with long–repressed feelings of teen angst and rebelliousness.

giving post-war kids a medium through which to express themselves. Teen emotions were being expressed in the words as well as the rhythms, while the music was more accessible for the fact that vocal and instrumental virtuosity were not prerequisites for performing it yourself. In the wake of Elvis Presley and Buddy Holly, guitar sales went through the roof and it was not long before tens of thousands of juvenile bands began springing up on both sides

of the Atlantic. Indeed, R&B-based skiffle music was a practical solution for kids who often did not have the funds to buy decent instruments; it also gave them great basic skills that would be useful in years to come.

As the 1950s gave way to the 1960s, white adults were still largely running the rock'n'roll scene, and a combination of social pressure and self-destructive circumstances helped to spell the end of the black-derived rock'n'roll. Chuck Berry and Jerry Lee Lewis were jailed, Little Richard joined the Church, Buddy Holly and Eddie Cochran were killed and Elvis Presley joined the US Army. These acts were replaced by lightweight, ballad-crooning artists: Frankie Avalon, Pat Boone, Ricky Nelson. Still, the era that coincided with Cold War crises and President Kennedy's tenure in the White House was not just about soapy ballads. It was also about the classic, three-minute pop songs that were being turned out from New York City's Brill Building; about a solo dance craze known as The Twist; about the innovative 'Wall-of-Sound' hits produced by wunderkind Phil Spector; about the non-stop flow of pulsating dance material from Motown's Hitsville facility in Detroit; and about the surf-and-hot-rod sounds emanating from Californian outfits such as The Beach Boys.

America had led the way with regard to popular music for much of the twentieth century, but things were about to change. Some British kids, whose lives had been irrevocably changed by rock'n'roll as well as R&B, were stamping their own distinctive style and personality on the music. When they transported it back across the Atlantic, the shock waves reverberated throughout the industry. The Beatles led the invasion, with their guitar-and-drums-based sound. R&B-influenced rockers, such as The Animals and The Rolling Stones, and mod outfits, such as The Who, provided contrast by way of their devil-may-care attitude and less clean-cut image. For a short time, many American artists found themselves having to imitate their Brit counterparts in order to make the charts. But by then, pop's fun and carefree attributes were charting a parallel but distinct course from the outspoken, introspective and experimental traits associated with the newly defined genre of rock music.

By the second half of the 1960s, many record buyers regarded pop as a tame and dated form of escapism for oldies and prepubescent teens. Rock, by comparison, provided a heavy dose of realism, serving as an introspective outlet for those who were no longer prepared to look at the world through rose-tinted spectacles but preferred to focus on hard-hitting topics rather than the innocent themes of boy-loves-girl, boy-loses-girl. John Lennon and his fellow Beatles led the way among the handful of artists who made

a successful transition from pop to rock. These included The Rolling Stones, The Yardbirds and The Who, who had already started out with a more aggressive rock sensibility. Add to them former folkies such as Bob Dylan, Jefferson Airplane and The Grateful Dead, and it was clear that, echoing the musical revolution that had exploded on both sides of the Atlantic a decade earlier, rock was the new voice of youth.

As the optimism of the Summer of Love gave way to late-1960s cynicism fuelled by civil unrest, anti-war riots and the hippy counterculture, so psychedelic and Eastern-tinged music were superseded by the vocal histrionics of Janis Joplin, as well as the blues-based hard rock of bands like Cream and The Jimi Hendrix Experience. Breaking with the pop tradition of radio-friendly three-minute songs, these acts indulged in far lengthier numbers that were often distinguished by extended instrumental solos. In so doing, they paved the way for subsequent decades' purveyors of heavy metal, progressive, jam and arena rock.

In a world where David Bowie and others were displaying a thespian-like theatricality, innovative psychedelia transmogrified into razzle-dazzle glam rock, people were pushing for bigger sounds onstage and in the studio, and concerts were being produced on an increasingly grand scale. It was as if excess was being equated with success and it was also evident that, 20 years after the likes of Elvis Presley and Jerry Lee Lewis had inspired teenagers, outraged parents and revolutionized Western culture, contemporary music had lost touch with its *raison d'être*.

No longer all that exciting, liberating or controversial, it promoted a musical virtuosity that was completely at odds with the easy-to-play, DIY appeal of rock'n'roll. Then along came punk rock, and for a brief time, the entire scene was given the shake up it so badly needed.

Between 1976 and 1978, the British punks in particular pumped up the aggression and devil-may-care attitude of their 1950s predecessors and quite literally spat in the face of authority and middle-class values. Drawing on often-limited musical talent, outfits such as The Sex Pistols and The Clash channelled their anger and energy into some blistering songs that once again helped to express the frustration and disenchantment of disaffected youth. The music was simply structured rock, and it had an invigorating effect on those who had grown tired of overblown, soulless material. Nevertheless, almost as soon as the punk movement became an international phenomenon, it was hijacked by kids from comfortable backgrounds who didn't have a clue about life on the streets, and undermined by some of the artists themselves, who embraced commercialism over independence when they signed with the major record labels.

Record companies attempted to broaden punk's appeal by associating more mainstream acts with the genre, resulting in a watered-down hybrid that was quickly dubbed 'new wave'. There were still traces of a surly attitude, and in the case of artists such as Elvis Costello there were clear musical skills, yet the spirit of punk had been laid to rest; for the next few years it would remain submerged while middle-of-the-road hard rockers and exotically attired 'new romantics' catered to the rapidly emerging MTV generation. Once easy to categorize, rock music continued to fragment throughout the 1980s and 1990s, with heavy metal splitting into subgenres ranging from thrash, speed and progressive to black, death and doom. At the same time, the indie/alternative tag served as a catch-all for a variety of styles, including that whose aesthetic was closest to that of vintage rock'n'roll, and which had the most far-reaching impact on the latter-day rock scene. Merging dissonant early 1970s heavy metal guitars with the hostile attitude, alienated lyrics and in-your-face music of punk, grunge rose to prominence with bands such as Soundgarden and reached its apotheosis with the more melodic approach of Nirvana and Pearl Jam in the early 1990s. It wasn't long before history repeated itself and grunge traded in its punk sensibilities for more widespread popularity.

At the start of the twenty-first century, rock music keeps subdividing and reinventing itself, continually absorbing influences from other musical spheres, and also looking to the past. The British art-rock banner once carried by Pink Floyd was re-hoisted by Coldplay and Radiohead. Dave Grohl of Nirvana fame seemed to have captured the

post-grunge *zeitgeist* with his new band Foo Fighters that became a great favourite at festivals, which were enjoying a renaissance in the new millennium. With acts such as The White Stripes emerging out of a new generation of bands playing a stripped down and back-to-basics version of guitar rock, it seems that there is still an appetite for good old rock'n'roll. And with artists such as The Rolling Stones and Bob Dylan still touring to sell-out crowds, and bands like Pink Floyd and Led Zeppelin reforming for one-off performances, it suggests that the cyclical nature of popular music will continue for the foreseeable future.

A-Z OF BANDS,

ACTS, ARTISTS

ABBA

VOCAL GROUP

The most commercially successful pop band of the 1970s, ABBA rose again in the 1990s when *ABBA Gold* (1992) revived their peerless singles' legacy, which has carried on ever since. ABBA were formed in 1972 in Stockholm, Sweden, by Benny Andersson (born Göran Bror Benny Andersson), Björn Ulvaeus and their girlfriends Frida Lyngstad (born Anni–Frid Lyngstad) and Agnetha Fältskog.

Andersson and Ulvaeus had been a songwriting partnership since 1969 after leaving respective bands The Hep Stars (Sweden's top pop band of the 1960s) and The Hootenanny Singers. Their girlfriends were both singers and Fältskog – who married Ulvaeus in 1971 – had had several solo hits. 'Waterloo' was picked as the 1974 Swedish Eurovision Song Contest entry and won, becoming a No. 1 single in the UK and around Europe. The girls' distinctive voices and harmonies and the boys' acute sense of pop melody and clever arrangements took 'SOS' to the US Top 20 in 1975. 'Mamma Mia' then sent them back to the top of the UK charts at the end of the year, although the US preferred 'I Do, I Do, I Do, I Do, I Do'.

The next two years saw ABBA dominate the British and European charts with a string of brilliantly conceived songs. 'Fernando', 'Dancing Queen', 'Knowing Me, Knowing You', 'The Name Of The Game' and 'Take A Chance On Me' all topped the UK charts while 'Money Money Money' made No. 3. They were all taken from No. 1 albums – *Greatest Hits* (1975), *Arrival* (1976) and *The Album* (1977).

In America, 'Dancing Queen' was their only No. 1, although 'Take A Chance On Me' got to No. 3 and 'Fernando', 'Knowing Me, Knowing You' and 'The Name Of The Game' made the Top 20. The rest of the world was falling under their spell, particularly Australia where the band toured in 1977. A film of this tour was released in 1978 as *Abba: The Movie*. The band maximized their revenue by making separate licensing agreements for each country.

TOP 100
ROCK ARTISTS

In October 1978 Andersson and Lyngstad got married, but ominously two months later Ulvaeus and Fältskog announced that they were separating. ABBA's personal relationships did not affect the songs, however. They built their own studio and the hits kept coming: 'Chiquitita' (all proceeds of which went to UNICEF), 'Does Your Mother Know', 'Voulez-Vous', 'Gimme! Gimme! Gimme! (A Man After Midnight)' and 'I Have A Dream' (1979), 'The Winner Takes It All' and 'Super Trouper' (1980), and 'Lay All Your Love On Me' and 'One Of Us' (1981). They played another world tour in 1979, which included America. When Andersson and Lyngstad filed for divorce in 1981 it was obvious that success was coming at a personal cost.

SOLO SUCCESS AND BEYOND

The group ceased after *The Visitors* (1981). There were solo albums from Lyngstad (who had an international hit with the Phil Collins-produced 'There's Something Going On' in 1982). Andersson and Ulvaeus continued to work together, collaborating with Tim Rice for the *Chess* musical.

The release of *ABBA Gold* sparked a major ABBA revival that raised the band to iconic status. The album topped the charts around the world, except in the US despite selling six million copies. In the UK it topped the charts three times in 1999 after the opening of *Mamma Mia*, the long-running musical based on ABBA songs. But despite the success of this and the Meryl Streep feelgood movie that followed in 2008, the original ABBA members have resisted all offers to reform.

GENRES

Pop, Glam Rock, Disco

ACTIVE YEARS

1972–83

CLASSIC RECORDINGS

'Waterloo', 'Mamma Mia', *Arrival*, 'Dancing Queen', 'Gimme! Gimme! Gimme! (A Man After Midnight)'

AC/DC

VOCAL/INSTRUMENTAL GROUP

AC/DC are a hard-rock quintet whose no-frills approach garnered them a huge following. They were formed in Sydney, Australia, in 1973 by expatriate Scottish brothers Angus and Malcolm Young (both guitar). Bon Scott became lead singer in 1974. After their first two albums were released only in Australia and New Zealand, the band moved to America. Here, their fifth album for Atlantic Records, *Highway To Hell* (1979), produced by Mutt Lange, established them in the big league, selling over six million copies. Its title track became a rock radio anthem.

When the hard-living Scott died from alcoholic poisoning in London in February 1980, he was replaced by Brian Johnson, former singer of glam rock band Geordie. The transition was seamless; AC/DC's first album with Johnson, *Back In Black* (1980), provided their only UK No. 1. With a revolving cast of drummers and bassists, AC/DC have stuck to a winning formula, eschewing the vagaries of fashion in favour of direct, audience-pleasing rock'n'roll. The 2008 release *Black Ice*, their first studio album for eight years, inspired an 18-month world tour. During this time the Recording Industry Association of America (RIAA) upgraded the group's US sales figures to 71 million, making them the fifth best-selling band and ninth best-selling artist in US history. The RIAA also certified *Back In Black*'s US sales as double diamond (20 million).

GENRES

Heavy Metal, Hard Rock, Rock'n'Roll

ACTIVE YEARS

1973–present

CLASSIC RECORDINGS

'It's a Long Way to the Top (If You Wanna Rock'n'Roll)', 'Highway To Hell', *Back In Black*, 'For Those About to Rock (We Salute You)'

AEROSMITH

VOCAL/INSTRUMENTAL GROUP

Aerosmith are the best-selling American rock band of all time, having sold more than 150 million albums worldwide. The heavy rock band is centred on the relationship between principal members Steven Tyler (vocals) and Joe Perry (guitar). The pair came together in Boston, Massachusetts, with Joey Kramer (drums), Brad Whitford (guitar) and Tom Hamilton (bass). Their first album *Aerosmith* (1973) was an immediate success, paving the way for the multi-platinum *Toys In The Attic* (1974) and *Rocks* (1975).

Antagonism between Tyler and Perry led to the latter's departure in 1980, to be replaced by Jimmy Crespo. Differences were set aside four years later when Perry returned to the fold. The band's profile was raised by the ground-breaking collaboration with rappers Run DMC on the single 'Walk This Way' in 1986, leading to a triumphant resurgence in Aerosmith's fortunes with *Permanent Vacation* (1987), *Pump* (1989) and *Get A Grip* (1993). Aerosmith were a key influence on 1990s American hard rock. More recently, Tyler's withdrawal from a South American tour planned for 2009 led to a year of disharmony in which Perry threatened to audition for a new singer, a move reminiscent of fellow US giants Journey and Steve Perry. Despite health problems, Tyler rejoined for 2010 dates, and the first album of original material for a decade was next on the agenda.

GENRES

Hard Rock, Heavy Metal, Blues Rock

ACTIVE YEARS

1970–present

CLASSIC RECORDINGS

'Dream On', *Toys In The Attic*, 'Walk This Way', *Rocks*, *Permanent Vacation*, *Pump*, *Get A Grip*

THE ALLMAN BROTHERS BAND
VOCAL/INSTRUMENTAL GROUP

A southern American blues–rock band comprising Duane Allman (guitar), Gregg Allman (vocals, organ), Dickey Betts (guitar, vocals), Berry Oakley (bass), Butch Trucks and Jai Johanny 'Jaimoe' Johanson (both drums), The Allman Brothers Band formed in Macon, Georgia in 1969.

The brothers had earlier recorded two albums as Hourglass, while Duane had also become a much–in demand session player known for his bottleneck guitar style. Indeed, he was the unofficial fifth member of Derek & The Dominos and played the memorable slide lick on 'Layla', which most people assumed was Eric 'Derek' Clapton. Gregg meanwhile, who shot himself in the foot in 1965 to avoid the Vietnam draft, was both a gravel–voiced vocalist and the band's main songwriter. The majority of the band's repertoire, however, consisted of blues standards and popular songs turned into instrumental tours de force by guitarists Duane and Dickey Betts. The late Otis Redding's manager Phil Walden was so impressed he came out of retirement to manage them.

HIGHS AND LOWS

The band's incendiary double lead guitar sound was best captured on *At Fillmore East* (1971), where songs like Gregg's 'Whipping Post' were elongated to take up a side of the vinyl. Betts claimed that 'if a tune is 20 minutes long as much as 10 minutes is going to be improvised'. And the framework was rarely overstretched. There was a fabulous freedom in recordings like *At Fillmore East* and *Eat A Peach* (the latter a 1973 double album that utilized some previously unreleased Fillmore tapes) that showed blues need not be a straitjacket.

The Allman Brothers Band took their outlaw image and lyrics to extremes. When they visited Britain to play the first open–air Knebworth Festival in 1974, the legendary status they enjoyed was due not only to their music

but also to the tragic loss of first Duane Allman (in 1971) and then Berry Oakley (1972) in separate motorcycle accidents. Both were 24 when they died, and Oakley's death happened just 1,000 yards from where Duane had perished.

Happily, the band returned to the stage on New Year's Eve 1972 with a gig at the Warehouse in New Orleans. With Lamar Williams as their new bass player they vowed that a double dose of tragedy wouldn't stop them becoming one of America's biggest attractions. The hockey and basketball stadiums beckoned, not to mention playing to 600,000 at the Watkins Glen Summer Jam in 1973, but the losses sustained in getting there would never be forgotten. One post-Duane album, 1973's *Brothers And Sisters*, delivered hits like 'Rambling Man' (a US No. 2 hit) and 'Jessica', the latter an instrumental that became the theme tune of BBC TV's *Top Gear*.

AN UNTIMELY END

Sadly The Allmans seemed determined not to enjoy their fame. Gregg's brief 1975 marriage to Cher combined with certain band members' insistence on self-indulgent solo projects diluted the appeal. Gregg's decision to testify against his roadie Scooter Herring in a 1976 drugs trial in return for immunity from prosecution proved to be the last straw. Fans and fellow band members revolted, and a split was inevitable. Latter-day keyboardist Chuck Leavell currently plays with The Rolling Stones, while other Allmans have sporadically re-formed. They were among the first bands to wave the Southern rock banner on the South's first label, Capricorn, leading the likes of Lynyrd Skynyrd, Molly Hatchet and Marshall Tucker towards the riches of the mainstream. But in truth the tragedies they survived weakened their legendary status.

GENRES

Southern Rock, Blues Rock, Blues, Jazz Fusion, Jam

ACTIVE YEARS

1969–76, 1978–82, 1989–present

CLASSIC RECORDINGS

At Fillmore East, 'In Memory Of Elizabeth Reed', 'Whipping Post', *Eat A Peach*, *Brothers And Sisters*, 'Ramblin' Man'

THE ANIMALS

VOCAL/INSTRUMENTAL GROUP

After million-selling 'The House Of The Rising Sun' in 1964, Tyneside's Eric Burdon (vocals), Hilton Valentine (guitar), Alan Price (organ and keyboards), Chas Chandler (bass) and John Steel (drums) racked up further international smashes as The Animals. By 1965, music press popularity polls had them breathing down the necks of The Beatles and The Rolling Stones. Price then left to pursue a solo career and was replaced by Dave Rowberry from The Mike Cotton Sound.

It was business as usual for The Animals until they disbanded after 1966's 'Don't Bring Me Down' fell from the Top 20. Burdon was persuaded to front a New Animals, who racked up hits of a psychedelic tinge like 'Monterey' and 'Sky Pilot' and briefly boasted future Police band member Andy Summers in their ranks. Their output was very under-rated outside the US. The old line-up reassembled for periodic reunion concerts and for two albums – 1976's *Before We Were So Rudely Interrupted* and, more notably, *Ark* in 1983, which they promoted – along with a re-released 'The House Of The Rising Sun' – on a world tour. Chandler died in 1996, but Burdon rocks on regardless, his bluesy rasp still one of rock's most distinctive voices.

GENRES

Blues Rock, R&B, Rock'n'Roll, Psychedelic Rock

ACTIVE YEARS

1962–66

CLASSIC RECORDINGS

'The House Of The Rising Sun', 'We've Gotta Get Out Of This Place', 'It's My Life', 'Don't Bring Me Down'

THE BAND

VOCAL/INSTRUMENTAL GROUP

The Band's debut LP, 1968's *Music From Big Pink*, was, like most of their later albums, a true blend of electric folklore nurtured over rough nights in Canadian palais with rock'n'roller Ronnie Hawkins before Robbie Robertson (guitar, vocals), Richard Manuel (piano, vocals), Rick Danko (bass, vocals), Garth Hudson (organ, saxophone) and Levon Helm (drums, vocals) landed a job backing Bob Dylan in 1965.

Their second album, simply titled *The Band* (1969), became not only a surprise US Top 10 hit but, equally importantly, a touchstone for the likes of Steve Marriott (with the original Humble Pie) and Eric Clapton, who sought to emulate their effortless, laid–back majesty. The album contained classics like 'The Night They Drove Old Dixie Down', 'Rag Mama Rag' and 'Up On Cripple Creek', the latter two sung by Helm. Subsequent albums each contained occasional Americana gems but inevitably lacked the first pair's refreshing consistency. Additionally, Robertson was singled out by the media as frontman, causing tensions in the ranks. The Band officially bowed out at *The Last Waltz*, a 1976 concert film that marked their official farewell to the road. Various re–groupings, all without Robertson, would persist until Manuel (1986) and finally Danko (1999) died.

GENRES

Rock'n'Roll, Country Rock, Folk Rock, Psychedelic Rock

ACTIVE YEARS

1964–76

CLASSIC RECORDINGS

Music From Big Pink, 'The Weight', *The Band, Stage Fright, The Last Waltz*

THE BEACH BOYS

VOCAL/INSTRUMENTAL GROUP

America's most successful pop group, graduating from fun-in-the-California-sun, surf and hot-rod songs to multi-textured, intricately arranged numbers of exquisite harmonic structure, The Beach Boys initially achieved fame with a line-up consisting of the Wilson brothers, Brian, Dennis and Carl, together with cousin Mike Love and high-school friend Al Jardine. Growing up in Hawthorne, Los Angeles, just miles from the Pacific, the Wilsons and Love were well versed in harmonizing together by the time Jardine joined the fold. Without any formal training, Carl took up the guitar, Brian and Jardine alternated on bass, Dennis drummed in rudimentary fashion and Love was the main lead vocalist.

Released on the tiny local Candix label in 1961, 'Surfin'' climbed to No. 75 on the *Billboard* chart and helped secure The Beach Boys a contract with Capitol Records. When Jardine quit to pursue a dentistry degree another friend, 15-year-old David Marks, helped record their first album, *Surfin' Safari*, released in late 1962 along with a single comprising the title track and, as its B-side, '409' which made the Top 20.

PRESSURE MOUNTS

Capitol began demanding new material at a frenetic rate, placing a huge burden on Brian and necessitating plenty of filler in order for The Beach Boys to record and release four more albums by the end of 1963. Still, there were numerous classics along the way, including 'Catch A Wave', 'Little Deuce Coupe', and the sublime harmony-laced ballads 'Surfer Girl' and 'In My Room'. All displayed Brian's abilities as a songwriter, arranger and producer.

Jardine reclaimed his job from Marks as The Beach Boys held their own against the onslaught of Beatlemania and the British Invasion through 1964. Several new albums, a string of infectious hit singles – 'Fun, Fun, Fun', chart-topper 'I Get Around' and 'Dance, Dance, Dance' – and beautifully composed, produced and performed tracks like

'Don't Worry Baby', 'The Warmth Of The Sun', 'Girls On The Beach' and 'All Summer Long' proved their worth. The pressure was too much for Brian, however, and that December, while on tour with the band, he suffered a nervous breakdown and quit the road for good.

While he was replaced on a permanent basis by multi-instrumentalist Bruce Johnston, Brian focused on his songwriting which, as illustrated by tracks like 'When I Grow Up (To Be A Man)' and the chart-topping 'Help Me, Rhonda', was moving into more contemplative and introspective areas. When the brothers' overbearing father Murry Wilson was fired as manager, Brian took the opportunity to employ the cream of L.A.'s session musicians to record backing tracks to his specifications. Love, Carl, Dennis and Jardine then added vocals. The results were self-evident, both in the consistent quality of material on 1965's *Today!* album, and the highly sophisticated production on one of Brian's masterpieces, 'California Girls', with its stunning harmonies and brilliant arrangement.

COMPETING WITH THE BEATLES

Simultaneously awed and inspired by The Beatles' *Rubber Soul* (1965), Brian immediately took it upon himself to outdo the compositional and recorded achievements of the Fab Four, and in collaboration with lyricist Tony Asher came up with some of his most beautiful and timeless material. Songs such as 'Wouldn't It Be Nice', 'God Only Knows', 'Caroline No', 'You Still Believe In Me', 'Don't Talk (Put Your Head On My Shoulder)' and 'I Just Wasn't Made For These Times' revealed not only the extent of Brian's talent as a writer and arranger but also a maturity that belied his 23 years. All appeared together, along with classic cuts like 'Sloop John B', on 1966's *Pet Sounds* album.

Hailed worldwide and a No. 2 best-seller in the UK, *Pet Sounds* was a surprising failure with the American public, which evidently still expected to hear songs about sun and surf. Brian then produced one of the all time great singles in 'Good Vibrations', an effects-filled track he withheld from *Pet Sounds* in order to spend six months (and $50,000) perfecting its intricately assembled, multi-sectional structure.

In the summer of 1966, spurred on by The Beatles' *Revolver* album, Brian embarked on what he intended to be his avant-pop masterpiece while himself ingesting copious amounts of marijuana and LSD. Van Dyke Parks was recruited to contribute offbeat, sometimes unfathomable lyrics, but results became fragmented and after 10 months' intense work, Brian shelved the now re-titled *SMiLE*.

A NEW CHAPTER

The Beach Boys soldiered on, often without their chief creative force. Some of the material intended for *SMiLE* – such as 'Heroes And Villains' – was either remixed or reworked for the moderate *Smiley Smile* (1967) LP, and although albums such as *Wild Honey* (1967), *Sunflower* (1970), *Surf's Up* (1971) and *Love You* (1977) would contain definite moments of magic (many still instigated by Brian), the band's ability to influence and inspire was a thing of the past. Its future lay mainly in dynamic concert performances, surviving even Dennis's alcohol and drug abuse and death in 1983 by drowning.

Carl's death from brain cancer in 1998 effectively put an end to The Beach Boys, yet Love and Johnston still tour with their own band under that banner. More surprisingly, Brian Wilson's live re-creation of *SMiLE* toured the world in 2004. A gig reuniting the survivors was planned to celebrate their fiftieth anniversary in 2011.

GENRES

Surf Rock, Pop, Psychedelic

ACTIVE YEARS

1961–present

CLASSIC RECORDINGS

'Surfin' Safari', 'I Get Around', 'Help Me Rhonda', 'California Girls', *Pet Sounds*, 'Good Vibrations'

THE BEATLES

VOCAL/INSTRUMENTAL GROUP

Consisting of John Lennon on rhythm guitar, Paul McCartney on bass, George Harrison on lead guitar and Ringo Starr on drums, The Beatles evolved from Lennon's school skiffle group, The Quarry Men, to become the most successful, acclaimed and influential act in the history of popular music. Born and raised in the seaport of Liverpool, John, Paul, George and Ringo had no formal musical education, yet were steeped in the traditions of British music hall, as well as the sounds of pre- and post-war popular music that emanated from the radio. In addition, the blues and country & western records local sailors brought home from their trips to America meant that the soon-to-be Fab Four absorbed an eclectic array of influences.

Lennon's Quarry Men, one of thousands of groups that sprang up all over Britain in the wake of the Lonnie Donegan-inspired skiffle boom, received a boost via the recruitment of the younger but more instrumentally adept Paul McCartney. George Harrison joined the fold in 1958.

THE EARLY YEARS

After a fallow period featuring few gigs and a revolving door of drummers, the summer of 1960 marked the first of several turning points for the band. Lennon had persuaded his art-college friend Stuart Sutcliffe to fill in on bass, and on the eve of an extended club engagement in Hamburg, West Germany, full-time drummer Pete Best arrived at last. It was in Hamburg that The Beatles really came of age during long, gruelling sessions onstage where they had to learn to improvise, extend their repertoire and really put on a show.

When John, Paul, George, Stuart and Pete made their reappearance on the Liverpool club circuit at the end of 1960, they were a local phenomenon, wowing audiences with their new powerhouse brand of rock'n'roll.

TOP 100
ROCK ARTISTS

Sutcliffe quit the group after a second Hamburg stint in the spring of 1961, preferring to remain there with his photographer girlfriend Astrid Kirchherr – he would tragically die of a brain haemorrhage the following year – with McCartney taking over on bass.

One of The Beatles' favoured venues was the Cavern Club, a dank and musty Liverpool warehouse cellar. In November 1961, local record retailer Brian Epstein witnessed one of the group's energetic Cavern Club performances, interspersing their musical numbers with onstage swearing, smoking and drinking. This was unconventional behaviour during an era of smooth, clean-cut pop idols. Epstein persuaded his charges that, if they wanted success, they would need to adopt a far more professional and disciplined approach. In return, he secured The Beatles more money and better bookings while doing the rounds of London record companies. The only one to show interest was EMI's small Parlophone label, run by George Martin. Intrigued as much by their personalities as their musical ability, Martin signed The Beatles. He was less than impressed with Pete's drumming, and on the eve of fame Best was replaced by Richard Starkey, better known as Ringo Starr, the sad-eyed, charismatic drummer with another well-liked Liverpudlian outfit, Rory Storm & The Hurricanes.

SUPERB SONGWRITING

Lennon and McCartney had written songs both separately and together, and while few had surpassed the standard of first single, 'Love Me Do' (1962), the pair now went into another gear, producing songs of incredible range and increasing sophistication. Infectious early hits such as 'Please Please Me', 'She Loves You' and 'I Want To Hold Your Hand' helped the band conquer Britain in 1963 amid hysterical fan scenes of what the press aptly termed 'Beatlemania'. Later hits such as 'A Hard Day's Night' (the title of their first, highly acclaimed film), 'Can't Buy Me Love' and 'I Feel Fine' saw them slay America and the rest of the world during the halcyon year of 1964.

As Beatlemania ran its course and the group members became jaded with the trappings of fame and non-stop concert, TV and radio appearances, they quit the road, withdrew to the EMI Studios on Abbey Road and embarked on the second and even more remarkable phase of their career. Between 1966 and 1969, drawing on personal experiences, socio-cultural influences, Harrison's immersion in Indian music and philosophy, and Lennon's prodigious

ingestion of mind–bending drugs, they produced recordings of breathtaking scope, originality and imagination that combined with technological innovation, and musical and (sometimes) lyrical sophistication.

A LASTING LEGACY

From the albums *Revolver* (1966), *Sgt Pepper's Lonely Hearts Club Band* (1967), *The Beatles* (a.k.a. *The White Album*, 1968) and *Abbey Road* (1969) to landmark singles like 'Eleanor Rigby', 'Strawberry Fields Forever', 'Hey Jude' and Harrison's 'Something', The Beatles created a body of work that, more than 35 years after the band's demise, still has a solid grip on the mass consciousness. To achieve this legacy, they overcame Brian Epstein's 1967 drug–overdose death and the subsequent bitter squabbles.

All four members enjoyed solo careers in the 1970s and beyond. Having decided to return to music after a four-year break, Lennon's life was cruelly cut short by an assassin's bullet in 1980. McCartney's Wings, which included first wife Linda, was, initially at least, a deliberately amateurish and spontaneous antidote to his superstar status while Harrison's spiritually inspired music never surpassed his 1970 triple album *All Things Must Pass* and transatlantic No. 1 hit single 'My Sweet Lord'. Ringo continues to tour the US singing his Beatles hits. He was also the voice of the children's TV show *Thomas The Tank Engine*.

GENRES

Pop, Rock

ACTIVE YEARS

1960–70

CLASSIC RECORDINGS

'Please Please Me', 'A Hard Day's Night', 'I Feel Fine', *Sgt Pepper's Lonely Hearts Club Band*, *The Beatles* (a.k.a. *The White Album*), 'Hey Jude', *Abbey Road*

THE BEE GEES

VOCAL GROUP

By adapting their songwriting and harmonies to different trends over four decades, The Bee Gees maintained a successful career. Gibb brothers – Barry and twins Robin and Maurice – moved to Australia with their parents in 1958 and landed a weekly spot on a TV show in 1960. Moving to the UK in 1967, their first single – the high-pitched ballad 'New York Mining Disaster 1941' – was a Top 20 hit in the UK and the US. It was the first of 10 over the next two years including 'To Love Somebody' and 'Massachusetts' (1967), 'Words' and 'I've Gotta Get A Message To You' (1968).

After that their career hit the doldrums until US producer Arif Mardin helped them latch onto the rising disco boom with US No. 1s 'Jive Talkin'' in 1975 and 'You Should Be Dancing in 1976'. In 1977 they wrote songs for movie *Saturday Night Fever*, whose soundtrack (1978) topped the US charts for 24 weeks and the UK charts for 18 weeks. After three more US No. 1 singles the hits tailed off, although they continued to write for Diana Ross ('Chain Reaction') and Kenny Rogers/ Dolly Parton ('Islands In The Stream'). Maurice's death in 2003 saw Barry and Robin retire the name, although they occasionally work together.

GENRES
Pop, Soft Rock, Disco

ACTIVE YEARS
1958–2003

CLASSIC RECORDINGS
'Massachusetts', 'Jive Talkin'', *Saturday Night Fever*, 'Stayin' Alive', *Spirits Having Flown*, 'Tragedy'

CHUCK BERRY

GUITAR, VOCALS

Charles Edward Anderson 'Chuck' Berry was born in St Louis, Missouri and began learning the guitar in his mid-teens. At 17 he was involved in a string of robberies that led to a jail sentence, from which he was released on his twenty-first birthday. On release Berry played pick-up gigs while studying to be a hairdresser and looking after his wife and children. On 30 December 1952, he got a call from piano-player Johnnie Johnson who had a gig at the Cosmopolitan Club in East St Louis. Berry was used to playing white bars, and started to introduce country songs alongside the blues and standards.

In early 1955, he saw Muddy Waters in Chicago and afterwards was advised to see Leonard Chess. Both Chess and bassist/fixer Willie Dixon were intrigued by the sound of Berry's 'Ida May', developed from country bopper Bob Wills's 'Ida Red'. The song became 'Maybellene' and was recorded at Chess Records on 21 May 1955. Around this time the band also stopped being The Johnnie Johnson Trio and became Chuck Berry's band. The song appealed to both races and stormed up all three American charts: pop, country and R&B.

YOUNG AT HEART

'Thirty Days', a hurriedly issued follow-up, did not fare so well, and it was not until mid-1956 that another classic, 'Roll Over Beethoven', breached the US Top 30. Berry's creativity was in full flow. After a slew of scintillating but hardly chart-busting singles, 'School Day' became a bona fide smash. It reached No. 3 in the US and gave Berry his first UK hit. Berry was in his thirties, but seemed to be able to describe teenage life to a tee. With his witty vignettes of American life, explored in verses dense with evocative imagery and metrical complexity, he was the first poet of the new sound; and his paean to the genre, 'Rock And Roll Music', became his next hit.

By this time Berry had bought his Club Bandstand and the land for Berry Park and set up Chuck Berry Music. He did not want to be cheated as he had been in the early days, though he was not averse to making sure he paid his backing musicians as little as possible. This included the loyal Johnnie Johnson, his former boss and, some say, co-composer of many of his songs.

After School Sessions was both Berry's and Chess Records' first LP, released in 1958, his best chart year by far. It also saw 'Sweet Little Sixteen' – with its list of place names guaranteeing sales in those locations – attaining No. 2 in the US, and No. 16, appropriately enough, in the UK. The semi-autobiographical 'Johnny B Goode' (the surname in honour of his birthplace on Goode Avenue, St Louis) came next, strolling to No. 8 in America. In 1959, his standards were just as high, but his chart placings began to slip. The extraordinarily strong pairing of 'Back In The USA' and 'Memphis, Tennessee' barely scraped into the Top 40. The answer to his own 'Johnny B Goode', entitled 'Bye Bye Johnny', had a prophetic ring. Berry had been harassed by the police for the last few years, but he did not help matters by bringing a 14-year-old Apache girl from Mexico to work at his St Louis club. A racist judge added to the problems, and after legal delays, Berry spent two more years in jail for transporting a minor for immoral purposes.

BACK ON TRACK

The Beatles, whose Hamburg sets were crammed with Berry originals, and The Rolling Stones, whose first single 'Come On' was a Chuck original, already knew all about him. An eponymous compilation released in 1963 spread the word further, going to No. 12 in Britain. 'Memphis, Tennessee' went to No. 6, and 'No Particular Place To Go' to No. 3. 'Nadine', 'Run, Rudolph, Run' and 'You Never Can Tell' also scored chart places. This burst of brilliance also revitalized his career in his homeland. In May 1964, Berry toured the UK to a tumultuous reception.

In June 1966, Berry signed with Mercury Records and the decline in his output was obvious. In fact, all the company really wanted him to do was re-record his classics so they had rights to the titles. Though *Chuck Berry In Memphis* (1967) was a half-decent set.

Berry began to play rock'n'roll revival shows, including Toronto, where Lennon and the Plastic Ono Band headlined. In 1970, Berry returned to Chess and in 1972 recorded his biggest, but by no stretch, finest hit. 'My Ding-A-Ling', a risqué novelty number, was a transatlantic No. 1.

BACK WHERE HE BEGAN

Berry produced little new material in the 1970s and ended the decade in jail again on tax charges. In 1986, he was in the first rank of artists to be inducted into the Rock And Roll Hall Of Fame. He was inducted by Keith Richards, who had based a career on Berry's guitar style, though that style, in turn, had been based on forefathers such as Charlie Christian and T-Bone Walker. The induction coincided with Berry's sixtieth birthday and Richards organized a huge celebratory bash, filmed in its entirety in the documentary *Hail! Hail! Rock'n'Roll*; a fascinating tribute to a great showman (when he felt like it) and the greatest lyricist of his era.

Chuck Berry played on into the new millennium, fronting local pick-up bands and duckwalking in a way that belied his 83 years – a true living legend of rock'n'roll.

GENRES

Rock'n'Roll, Blues

ACTIVE YEARS

1955–present

CLASSIC RECORDINGS

'Maybellene', 'Roll Over Beethoven', 'Johnny B Goode', 'No Particular Place To Go', 'My Ding-A-Ling'

BLACK SABBATH

VOCAL/INSTRUMENTAL GROUP

Pioneers of heavy metal, Black Sabbath hailed from Birmingham, England and comprised John 'Ozzy' Osbourne (vocals), Tony Iommi (guitar), Terence 'Geezer' Butler (bass) and Bill Ward (drums). Over 10 years and half a dozen or so classic albums, they are the band that almost single-handedly invented the term 'heavy metal'. Their self-styled Satanic image was always tongue-in-cheek, but their brain-crunching 1970 anthem 'Paranoid', their second album's title track, has gone down as one of the greatest rock songs ever recorded. Sabbath's music featured doom-laden lyrics intoned by Osbourne through a curtain of hair and set to down-tuned guitar.

Never taken seriously at the time by either their record labels or the critics, Black Sabbath's riff-dominated, black-hearted rock found immediate favour with teenage male fans who bought their records by the million. However, by the end of the 1970s, as Sabbath fell into a mire of drug addiction and management problems, Osbourne was ousted from the band he helped start.

BACK ON TOP

Down but not out, Ozzy's flagging career was swiftly turned around by Sharon Arden, who became his manager and then his wife. Hooking up with American guitar-wizard Randy Rhoads, Ozzy was soon back on top with a clutch of well-received solo albums such as *Blizzard Of Ozz* (1980) and *Diary Of A Madman* (1981). Rhoads tragically died in a plane accident in 1982 and, in the aftermath, Ozzy's life once again began to spiral out of control. Happily this was resolved with Sharon's help and, as well as continuing to record and perform, he has lent his name to the annual Ozzfest heavy metal festivals. He became an unlikely reality TV star when the Osbourne family was filmed for an MTV series that won the highest ratings in the channel's history.

After a decade of hard-rock domination, Sabbath had been determined to keep their crown despite Osbourne's absence. Ex-Rainbow singer Ronnie Dio was an inspired choice and 1980's *Heaven And Hell* proved a largely ignored classic. Ex-Deep Purple vocalist Ian Gillan on the other hand, was a disastrous choice for 1983's *Born Again*. Tony Martin and the returning Dio served until Osbourne, who renounced drink and drugs for good in 1991, finally rejoined his colleagues in 1997. It was the first time Ozzy, Tony, Geezer and Bill had shared a stage (15 minutes at Live Aid aside) since 1979. A string of sell-out performances and a 1998 live album, *Reunion*, preceded a spell of studio activity, and the on-off alliance continued through most of the first decade of the new millennium. Osbourne and Iommi did however resort to law to decide ownership of the Sabbath name. An out-of-court agreement was reached.

The Dio-Butler-Iommi-Vinnie Appice line-up that cut *Heaven And Hell* started playing festivals under that name in 2006 to avoid any confrontation with Osbourne. They also cut a new album, *The Devil You Know* (2009), but Dio's death the following year ended this sub-chapter of the Sabbath story.

SABBATH'S LEGACY

Black Sabbath have been hugely influential, arguably far more so than their more critically lauded contemporaries Led Zeppelin. Metallica, Venom, Judas Priest, Faith No More, Alice In Chains ... the list of bands to have taken inspiration from Sabbath's golden period is endless. It's just unfortunate that they peaked so early. *Rolling Stone* magazine said second album *Paranoid* (1970) 'changed music forever' and called the band 'The Beatles of heavy metal'. It was recorded the year The Beatles split.

GENRES

Heavy Metal, Rock, Blues Rock

ACTIVE YEARS

1968–2006

CLASSIC RECORDINGS

Black Sabbath, Paranoid, 'Paranoid', *Master Of Reality, Vol. 4, Reunion*

BLUR

VOCAL/INSTRUMENTAL GROUP

Formed at London's Goldsmiths College, Damon Albarn (vocals), Graham Coxon (guitar), Alex James (bass) and Dave Rowntree (drums) tuned into the vibe generated by The Stone Roses with anthems 'She's So High' and 'There's No Other Way'. Although *Leisure* (1991) showed a band adept at updating 1960s pop, *Modern Life Is Rubbish* (1993) revealed depth. Then, with the release of infectious electro single 'Boys And Girls' and the cockney swagger of 'Parklife', Blur found themselves the leaders of the 'Britpop' movement. *Parklife* (1994) and *The Great Escape* (1995) cemented their reputation. Rivalry with Oasis was ill timed, although taking a more loud and experimental approach on *Blur* (1997) and *13* (1999) displayed greater musical maturity without losing sales or fans. Coxon departed to concentrate upon a solo career in 2002.

Albarn's desire for wider experimentation and collaboration found full flower in the Gorillaz project, but Blur reformed with their original four-piece line-up in 2009. Gigs including a Glastonbury Festival headline were the first in nine years and 'healed deep wounds', Albarn said. Recorded in London in April 2010, single 'Fool's Day' was the first song the quartet had made together since the album *Think Tank* (2003) and was recorded especially for Record Store Day.

GENRES

Britpop, Indie Rock

ACTIVE YEARS

1989–2003, 2009–present

CLASSIC RECORDINGS

'There's No Other Way', *Parklife*, 'Girls & Boys', *The Great Escape*, 'Country House', *Blur*, *13*

BON JOVI

VOCAL/INSTRUMENTAL GROUP

Bon Jovi were formed in 1983 in New Jersey by singer Jon Bon Jovi, guitarist Richie Sambora, keyboard player David Bryan, bassist Alec John Such and drummer Tico Torres. They were America's leading hard rock band in the 1980s but, by combining their musical aggression with catchy pop songs, they achieved universal appeal.

The make-or-break third album, *Slippery When Wet* (1986), stormed to the top of the US charts, propelled by two No. 1 singles – 'You Give Love A Bad Name' and 'Livin' On A Prayer' (both co-written by Desmond Child). They repeated the formula with even greater success on *New Jersey* (1988). It was a No. 1 album in the UK and the US where it topped the charts for four weeks, providing five Top 10 singles, including two No. 1s: 'Bad Medicine' (also co-written by Child) and 'I'll Be There For You'. The band capitalized with a gruelling American and international touring schedule that included headlining the UK Monsters Of Rock Festival at Castle Donington in 1987 and the Moscow Music Peace Festival in 1989. After a four-year hiatus, *Keep The Faith* (1992), produced by Bob Rock, redefined their sound. Another four-year break preceded *Crush* (2000). No longer innovators, Bon Jovi nevertheless retain their enormous popularity with male and female pop and rock fans.

GENRES

Rock, Hard Rock, Glam Rock

ACTIVE YEARS

1983–present

CLASSIC RECORDINGS

Slippery When Wet, 'Livin' On A Prayer', *New Jersey*, 'Bad Medicine', *Keep The Faith*, 'Always', 'It's My Life'

DAVID BOWIE

VOCALS

One of the great chameleon figures in rock, David Bowie (born David Robert Jones) has also been among the most influential. His earliest records with The King Bees, The Mannish Boys and The Lower Third were unsuccessful, but in 1966 he changed his name to David Bowie and combined his songwriting with an interest in stage and visual arts. However, it was not until 1969 that Bowie caught the British public's imagination with the quirky 'Space Oddity', which became a Top 5 hit soon after the first manned moon landing. Despite fuelling publicity with his androgynous image, Bowie's career continued to stutter with *The Man Who Sold The World* (1971) and *Hunky Dory* (1971) until he created the messianic rock star character Ziggy Stardust.

A STAR IS BORN

A glam-rock concept album, *The Rise And Fall Of Ziggy Stardust And The Spiders From Mars* (1972) formed the basis of a theatrical live show and was a Top 5 UK album. It was a hugely influential project and tracks like 'Ziggy Stardust', 'Moonage Daydream', 'Rock & Roll Suicide' and 'Suffragette City' have become classics. Bowie declared himself a bisexual around this time, and the controversy he created was stoked by antics such as kissing guitarist Mick Ronson on TV. Such was the interest in Bowie that *Hunky Dory* was revived and got to No. 3, while 'Life On Mars', perhaps his most impressive single, became a hit. His band – Mick Woodmansey (drums), Trevor Bolder (bass) and especially Mick Ronson (guitar, keyboards, vocals) – were dependable sidekicks.

Aladdin Sane, produced by Tony Visconti who played a significant role in most of Bowie's albums through the 1970s, topped the UK charts in 1973. But just weeks later – on 3 July 1973 – Bowie dramatically killed off the catsuited, flame-haired Ziggy persona live on stage in London, a performance later released on video/DVD.

After an interlude with *Pin-Ups* (1973), a covers album, Bowie returned with *Diamond Dogs* (1974). The album's bleak, Orwellian theme and the extravagant stage show he devised gave Bowie his American breakthrough, encouraging him to relocate there. Another stylistic switch based around the soul sound of Philadelphia completed Bowie's American triumph with *Young Americans* (1975). This album gave him a US No. 1 single with 'Fame' (co-written with John Lennon).

A MAN OF MANY TALENTS

By *Station To Station* (1976) Bowie's stage persona had metamorphosed into the 'Thin White Duke'. During this hectic period, Bowie also found time (with assistance from Ronson) to produce seminal albums by Lou Reed (*Transformer*, 1972) and Iggy Pop & The Stooges (*Raw Power*, 1973), write and produce Mott The Hoople's 'All The Young Dudes', and star in the film *The Man Who Fell To Earth* (1976). Later in 1976, frazzled from the perks and pressures of fame, Bowie retreated to seclusion in Berlin, studying art and working with pioneering electronic sound musician Brian Eno. The resulting *Low* (1977) was another radically different musical direction, exploring new instrumental and vocal sounds. It was the first of a trilogy with *Heroes* (1977) and *Lodger* (1979). His reputation ensured their success although some fans and critics were getting confused.

Bowie relocated to New York to record the paranoid *Scary Monsters* (1980), updating 'Space Oddity' with 'Ashes To Ashes'. He also collaborated with Queen for their 'Under Pressure' hit and Bing Crosby for the 'Peace On Earth'/'Little Drummer Boy' single, as well as taking the lead role in Broadway play *The Elephant Man* and writing film themes and soundtracks for *Christiane F* (1981, in which he also appeared) and *Cat People* (1982).

BACK TO THE MAINSTREAM

Bowie returned to the mainstream with *Let's Dance* (1983), produced by Chic's Nile Rodgers. This album yielded three international hits – 'China Girl', 'Modern Love' and 'Let's Dance', all with innovative videos, and prompted the successful Serious Moonlight world tour. This would prove his commercial peak, but turned off a significant number of his 1970s fans. Lead guitar was contributed by his new discovery Stevie Ray Vaughan, though the Texan declined to tour.

For the rest of the decade Bowie divided his time between: music – *Tonight* (1984) and *Never Let Me Down* (1987); duetting with Mick Jagger on 'Dancing In The Street' for Live Aid; acting (*Merry Christmas Mr Lawrence*, *Into The Night*, *Absolute Beginners*, *Labyrinth*); and soundtracks *The Falcon And The Snowman* (1985), *When The Wind Blows* (1986).

UPDATED SOUNDS

In 1989 Bowie formed a band called Tin Machine with the rhythm section from Iggy Pop's band and made two self–titled, rock–oriented albums. But their appeal was limited and he returned to his solo career, and producer Nile Rodgers, for the electro–dance styled *Black Tie White Noise* (1993). He continued to experiment with modern musical styles, drawing on industrial rock for *Outside* (1995) with Eno returning as producer and incorporating jungle beats on *Earthling* (1997). *Hours* (1999, made available as a download before the CD was released), *Heathen* (2002), with Tony Visconti back as producer, and *Reality* (2003) found Bowie in relaxed form, taking facets of his earlier career and updating them. That said, he has been notoriously shy of playing his older hits and, when he does, they are often radically rearranged.

David Bowie remains an icon and few rock acts of the past 30 years have been unaffected by his legacy. He has sold an estimated 136 million albums over the course of his 45–year career, and ranks among the 10 best–selling acts in UK pop history. He is currently married to Somali–born supermodel Iman, while his first marriage to the outrageous American Angie Bowie produced a son, Zowie. As Duncan Jones, he is now a successful movie director.

GENRES

Rock, Glam Rock, Art Rock, Soul

ACTIVE YEARS

1964–present

CLASSIC RECORDINGS

'Space Oddity', *Aladdin Sane*, *Diamond Dogs*, *Young Americans*, *Let's Dance*, 'Let's Dance', 'China Girl'

JAMES BROWN

VOCALS

Like many early soul stars James Brown (born in South Carolina) came to music through singing at his local church. He had his first success as frontman of The Famous Flames with the gospel R&B hit 'Please Please Please' in 1956. When 1958's 'Try Me' hit the R&B No. 1 spot, the floodgates opened with more entries on the R&B charts than anyone else, and more on the US pop charts than anyone but Elvis.

Unlike Presley, who sold his soul to Hollywood and had to regain his throne, Brown, who also began his run of hit records in the mid-1950s, never stopped working. His career took him around the world, from entertaining troops in Vietnam to heading the bill at the Montreux Jazz Festival on three occasions, and earned him many titles – 'The Hardest Working Man in Show Business', 'The Godfather of Soul' and 'The Minister of the New New Super Heavy Funk' being just three.

A FORMIDABLE LIVE ACT

The Flames became part of The James Brown Revue: an all-singing, all-dancing spectacle that played to capacity in black venues throughout America. The Revue had its own backing band, The JBs, and with them Brown began to make the transition from doo-wop pop to a tougher R&B sound. It was with The Revue that he earned and adopted the title 'Hardest Working Man in Show Business', reportedly losing 7lbs a night in perspiration through his energized performances. At the same time The JBs built a name as the tightest rhythm section around. A formidable live act, they were captured on *Live At The Apollo*, recorded in 1962 in Harlem at Brown's own expense; his label did not believe live albums sold. The album went to No. 2 in the US charts, an unprecedented crossover for an R&B act, selling over a million copies. It remains the first stop for anyone wanting an insight into the sheer passion and energetic professionalism through which James Brown established himself.

TOP 100
ROCK ARTISTS

The work he put into his stage act, with knee–drops, twists, turns, shimmies and even a staged collapse – Brown's entourage carrying him off, only for him to make an heroic return to thunderous applause – had paid rich dividends. Brown was also refining a vocal technique of chants and shouts as much as melody, and a musical form using more and more complex rhythms and riffs. The 1964 LP *Out Of Sight*, whose title track, a jazz–organ and brass groove with choppy guitar, was another R&B No. 1. With it, James Brown invented funk.

Reinvigorated by a new recording contract in 1965 and a revised JBs line–up (led by saxophonist Pee Wee Ellis), his next single 'Papa's Got A Brand New Bag' was a worldwide hit, earning Brown his first Grammy. The follow–up 'I Got You (I Feel Good)' cemented the deal, reaching No. 3 and laying the foundation for frequent US pop listings and almost uninterrupted presence in the R&B charts until 1970. A run of five big hits was completed by 'It's A Man's Man's Man's World', (1966), 'Cold Sweat' (1967) and 'I Got The Feeling' (1968).

SAY iT LOUD

Brown's success as a black businessman and superstar made him a role model for the African–American community. Hits from this time such as 'Say It Loud (I'm Black And I'm Proud)' from 1968 address the social and racial concerns of black youth. In April 1969, when race riots broke out in 30 US cities following the assassination of Martin Luther King, James Brown made a national TV address to appeal for calm, which received a ceremonial letter of gratitude from a grateful White House.

In 1971, Brown once again revised The JBs. The new line–up led by trombonist Fred Wesley played a deeper funk than ever, Brown's vocal output becoming ever more abstract and stylized. He sold millions of records, although with less crossover success. The JBs themselves had a successful parallel recording career with funk jams like 'Doing It To Death' (1973). Many former JBs (including bassist Bootsy Collins) graduated to George Clinton's Parliament–Funkadelic stable. There they would define funk in the 1970s just as they had invented it in the 1960s.

By 1975, both Brown and his band were running out of steam, and a new wave of funk was lapping at their heels led by Clinton, Kool & The Gang and others. Brown was also facing financial and personal difficulties, and attempts to update his sound were less than convincing. A cameo role in the 1980 film *The Blues Brothers*, however, returned him to mainstream attention, triggering a re-evaluation of his career and a revival of the epithet, 'The Godfather of Soul'. His comeback eventually saw 1986 single 'Living In America' make the UK and US Top 10s.

REVIVAL OF FORTUNE

That year he was one of the inaugural inductees to the Rock And Roll Hall Of Fame. Just as his fortunes were being revived, his personal life disintegrated again, and 1988 saw James Brown arrested five times on drugs and assault charges, and eventually sentenced to six years in prison. When he emerged on parole two years later, it was to a hip-hop world in which his back catalogue was the primary source for a new generation of funk-hungry DJs looking for a good groove to sample.

The award of a Lifetime Achievement Grammy in 1992 was well deserved. No longer an innovator himself, James Brown continued to inspire others with his energetic performances up until his death on 25 December 2006.

GENRES

R&B, Funk, Soul

ACTIVE YEARS

1956–2006

CLASSIC RECORDINGS

Live At The Apollo, 'Papa's Got A Brand New Bag', 'I Got You (I Feel Good)', *The Godfather: The Very Best Of James Brown*

THE BYRDS
VOCAL/INSTRUMENTAL GROUP

Jim (later Roger) McGuinn, David Crosby and Gene Clark were all seasoned folk musicians when, inspired by the sounds of the 'British Invasion', they teamed up in Los Angeles in early 1964 to form an acoustic folk-pop group called The Jet Set. Chris Hillman joined on bass though he had never played the instrument, while conga player Michael Clarke filled the drum stool. A group 'pilgrimage' to see *A Hard Day's Night* determined both the appearance and sound of the renamed Byrds.

McGuinn was the only member to appear on their version of Bob Dylan's 'Mr Tambourine Man', rearranged to Beatle-ish 4/4 time, which was a transatlantic smash in the summer of 1965. The 1966 single 'Eight Miles High' heralded in the era of psychedelic rock, although co-composer Clark quit the band shortly thereafter. It was The Byrds' last Top 20 US single, but they continued to enjoy success with the innovative *Fifth Dimension* (1966) and *Younger Than Yesterday* (1967) albums. In 1967 Crosby and Clarke departed, leaving McGuinn and Hillman to play on with new musicians including Gram Parsons, with whom they cut the first major country rock album, *Sweetheart Of The Rodeo*, in 1968. By 1973, following a one-album reunion of the original quintet, The Byrds were no more.

GENRES

Folk Rock, Psychedelic Rock, Country Rock

ACTIVE YEARS

1964–73

CLASSIC RECORDINGS

Mr Tambourine Man, Turn! Turn! Turn!, 'Eight Miles High', *Fifth Dimension, Younger Than Yesterday, Sweetheart Of The Rodeo*

JOHNNY CASH
GUITAR, SINGER/SONGWRITER

Johnny Cash was an inspiration to many in a career that spanned nearly five decades and transcended genres. His songwriting and bass-baritone vocals made him a multi-million-selling artist and icon, ensuring he kept performing right up to his death in 2003.

After serving in the United States Air Force, Arkansas-born Cash formed a trio with Luther Perkins (guitar) and Marshall Chapman (bass). Auditioning for Sam Phillips at Sun Records in Memphis, Cash soon turned from gospel to rockabilly and scored more than 20 US country hits and several US pop hits. In late 1958 he signed with Columbia/CBS and became one of the biggest country music attractions, remaining with the label until 1987. Cash became an American treasure during the 1960s, especially after recording live albums at *Folsom Prison* (1968) and *San Quentin* (1969), which both went triple platinum. In 1968, he married June Carter (of The Carter Family), and they fronted a hugely popular live revue for many years. After 1976, further mainstream success seemed an impossibility, until Rick Rubin offered to produce him. The resulting *American Recordings* (1994) was the first of four Grammy-winning albums on Rubin's label. Cash's daughter, Rosanne, keeps the family name alive, while Johnny was the subject of an Oscar-winning Hollywood film in 2005. *I Walk The Line*, starred Joaquin Phoenix as 'The Man in Black'.

GENRES

Country, Rock'n'Roll, Folk, Gospel, Blues

ACTIVE YEARS

1954–2003

CLASSIC RECORDINGS

'Folsom Prison Blues', 'I Walk The Line', 'Ring Of Fire', *At Folsom Prison*, *At San Quentin*, 'A Boy Named Sue', *American Recordings*

CHICAGO

VOCAL/INSTRUMENTAL GROUP

Starting life as politically savvy jazz-rockers Chicago Transit Authority, the horn-backed septet fronted by bassist-vocalist Peter Cetera and keyboardist-vocalist Robert Lamm released a series of albums whose titles were denoted by roman numerals. They were fashionably outspoken critics of authority in the Vietnam era, but also followed an eclectic musical path with free-form instrumentals and lengthy jazz/classical-inspired tracks alongside the singles.

Chicago morphed dramatically into soft-rock balladeers in the mid-1970s, thanks to the transatlantic chart-topping 'If You Leave Me Now' (1976). Two years later they split with manager/producer James William Guercio, while that same year guitarist Terry Kath fatally shot himself. Chicago continued on a new label (Warners, moving from CBS) and with a new producer (David Foster). Many buyers would not have connected the smooth ballads like 'Hard To Say I'm Sorry' (1982) with the brash, brassy early hits like '25 Or 6 To 4' (1970), but the change of musical direction ensured the band played on with many a personnel change into the new millennium. Even Cetera's departure in 1985 failed to derail them. Over the course of their career they have released five US No. 1 albums and have had 21 Top 10 hit singles.

GENRES

Jazz Rock, Hard Rock, Soft Rock, Pop

ACTIVE YEARS

1967–present

CLASSIC RECORDINGS

Chicago II, '25 Or 6 To 4', 'If You Leave Me Now', *Chicago 16*, 'Hard To Say I'm Sorry', *Chicago 17*, 'You're The Inspiration'

TOP 100
ROCK ARTISTS

ERIC CLAPTON

GUITAR, SINGER/SONGWRITER

Few guitarists have proved more popular role models than Eric Clapton. Ever since he burst onto the scene with The Yardbirds in late 1963, guitarists have been watching how and what he plays. Eighteen-year-old Eric Patrick Clapp (his given name) quit The Yardbirds in 1965 after hit 'For Your Love', believing The Yardbirds had strayed too far from the pure blues direction he favoured. British blues legend John Mayall then recruited Clapton for his own Bluesbreakers, with whom Eric reached the brink of superstardom during his one-album stay.

After 18 tumultuous months in Cream, Clapton renounced the spotlight for less high-profile stays with Delaney & Bonnie, Blind Faith (a brief supergroup with Steve Winwood) and Derek & The Dominos before commencing a solo career in 1970. He has followed his own light ever since, topping the US chart in 1974 covering Bob Marley's 'I Shot The Sheriff', but usually content to chug along in an easygoing AOR (album-oriented rock) vein. Clapton returned to pure blues again in 1994 with *From The Cradle*, but has since shared the spotlight with Jeff Beck (his Yardbirds successor), J.J. Cale, B.B. King and Steve Winwood on albums and tours that sell to would-be six-stringers of all ages.

GENRES

Blues, Blues Rock, Hard Rock, Psychedelic Rock

ACTIVE YEARS

1963–present

CLASSIC RECORDINGS

Bluesbreakers With Eric Clapton, Disraeli Gears, 'Crossroads', 'Layla', 461 Ocean Boulevard, Unplugged, From The Cradle

THE CLASH

VOCAL/INSTRUMENTAL GROUP

If The Sex Pistols were the face of UK punk, The Clash were the soul. The band was formed in the summer of 1976 by guitarist Mick Jones and bassist Paul Simonon after their proto-punk band, London SS, broke up. They recruited guitarist Keith Levene and drummer Terry Chimes before luring singer/guitarist Joe Strummer from pub rock band the 101ers. Their first gig was an unannounced support slot with The Sex Pistols in Sheffield. After five gigs Levine was fired and Terry Chimes followed early in 1977, having already recorded their debut album. His replacement was Topper Headon.

The Clash (1977) was one of the definitive punk albums featuring the anthem 'White Riot' and caustic rockers 'London's Burning', 'Janie Jones' and 'I'm So Bored With The USA'. CBS did not release the album in America although it sold an unprecedented 100,000 on import. After the White Riot UK tour, the band released a clutch of singles – 'Complete Control' (produced by Lee Perry), 'Clash City Rockers' and '(White Man) In Hammersmith Palais'.

SEEKING SUCCESS

Give 'Em Enough Rope (1978) entered the UK charts at No. 2 and gave them their first Top 20 single with 'Tommy Gun'. However, despite two successful American tours the album failed to chart in the US, as had been the aim in picking Blue Oyster Cult producer Sandy Pearlman. Switching producers again to R&B connoisseur Guy Stevens, The Clash went into creative overdrive for the eclectic but stylish double album *London Calling* (1979). This time they cracked the US Top 30 and had a hit single with 'Train In Vain'. They over-reached their creativity on the self-produced triple album *Sandinista!* (1980), which made the US Top 30 but only scraped into the UK Top 20.

Combat Rock (1982), produced by veteran Glyn Johns (Rolling Stones, Who, Eagles), refocused their energy with a big rock sound. They recaptured their best songwriting on 'Rock The Casbah' (their only US Top 10 hit),

'Straight To Hell' and 'Should I Stay Or Should I Go'. But Headon was fired for continued heroin use and the band toured stadiums with The Who with Chimes back on drums. In September 1983 Strummer and Simonon fired Jones who had 'drifted apart from the original idea of The Clash'. A new Clash featuring guitarists Vince White and Nick Sheppard toured America and Europe in 1984 but *Cut The Crap* (1985) served only to prove that the band had lost their way. Strummer and Simonon broke up The Clash early in 1986.

SUBSEQUENT SOLO PROJECTS

Jones had formed Big Audio Dynamite with film director/DJ Don Letts and Strummer joined him, co–producing and writing songs for their second album, *10 Upping Street* (1986). His subsequent solo career encompassed acting (*Mystery Train*), soundtracks (*Straight To Hell, Sid And Nancy*), producing The Pogues and various band projects including Latino Rockabilly War and The Mescaleros.

The posthumous legacy of The Clash continued to grow. *The Story Of The Clash Volume 1* (1988) made the UK Top 10. In 1991 the reissued 'Should I Stay Or Should I Go' gave them the UK No. 1 hit they had failed to achieve during their career. *From Here To Eternity: Live* (1999) was another UK Top 20 album. They continued to resist lucrative offers to reform right up until the sudden death of Joe Strummer from a heart attack on 22 December 2002.

GENRES

Punk Rock

ACTIVE YEARS

1976–86

CLASSIC RECORDINGS

The Clash, 'White Riot', 'Tommy Gun', *London Calling, Combat Rock*, 'Should I Stay Or Should I Go', 'Rock The Casbah'

COLDPLAY

VOCAL/INSTRUMENTAL GROUP

Coldplay were formed in London in 1996 by college friends Chris Martin (vocals), Jonny Buckland (guitar), Will Champion (drums) and Guy Berryman (bass). They impressed UK label Parlophone with the self-funded *Safety EP* CD (1998) and, after university responsibilities were fulfilled, the band signed a then-massive five-album deal.

Parachutes, Coldplay's 2000 album debut, found band and Martin in good voice, and hot singles 'Yellow' and 'Trouble' gained exposure on a worldwide scale. Intense touring saw confidence grow, while Martin's profile soared with his marriage to movie star Gwyneth Paltrow in 2003. *A Rush Of Blood To The Head*, which arrived in 2002, was full of much the same balladry and sly musicianship as its predecessor, but *X&Y* (2005) was more experimental. During the same year the band headlined Glastonbury and played the London leg of the Live 8 concerts. Released in June 2008, fourth album *Viva La Vida* topped the UK album chart after just three days' sales. Its title track became the band's first US No. 1, and it was clear their success story was set to continue.

GENRES

Indie, Alternative Rock

ACTIVE YEARS

1996-present

CLASSIC RECORDINGS

Parachutes, 'Yellow', 'Trouble', *A Rush Of Blood To The Head*, 'In My Place', 'Clocks', *X&Y*, 'Speed Of Sound', 'Fix You', *Viva La Vida*

SAM COOKE

VOCALS

With his pure, sweet voice, sound business awareness and keen social concerns, Sam Cooke was a key figure in the early development of soul and pop. He was already a star as a member of gospel group The Soul Stirrers when he was sacked in 1956 for releasing a secular solo single. He launched his solo career with a run of exquisite romantic ballads including 'You Send Me' and '(What A) Wonderful World'. A deal with RCA followed, which led to his own label and publishing house. A series of finely crafted pop songs such as 'Chain Gang' and 'Bring It On Home To Me' won him two separate audiences: white teenagers (RCA's target) and black listeners of all ages (to whom he was a role model). In 1963, Dylan's protest songs encouraged him to address civil-rights issues. That year Cooke recorded the majestic gospel spiritual 'A Change Is Gonna Come', which became a posthumous hit after his murder in 1964.

Cooke's influence has been a lasting soul legacy. Rod Stewart has recorded several of his boyhood idol's songs, while other notable cover versions have been recorded by Southside Johnny, Cat Stevens and Bobby Womack, who was signed to Cooke's SAR label with The Valentinos.

GENRES

R&B, Soul, Gospel, Pop

ACTIVE YEARS

1950–64

CLASSIC RECORDINGS

'You Send Me', '(What A) Wonderful World', 'Chain Gang', 'Bring It On Home To Me', 'A Change Is Gonna Come'

ELVIS COSTELLO

GUITAR, VOCALS

One of the new wave's most celebrated songwriters, Costello (born Declan Patrick MacManus) initially portrayed himself as an angry, revenge-obsessed young man before steadily maturing into a genre-straddling elder statesman. His cheeky appropriation of the name 'Elvis' was in tune with the iconoclastic mood of 1977, when his debut album *My Aim Is True* was released. Temporary backing band Clover were superseded by The Attractions – Bruce Thomas (bass), Steve Nieve (real name Nason, keyboards) and Pete Thomas (drums) – and their early work together, *This Year's Model* (1978) and *Armed Forces* (1979), established Costello as a major artist. *Get Happy* (1980) embraced soul music whilst an album of country covers, *Almost Blue* (1981), signalled expansive musical horizons.

Costello went on to work in a variety of genres and with various collaborators. These include The Brodsky (string) Quartet, songwriter Burt Bacharach, opera singer Anne-Sofie von Otter and New Orleans musician Allen Toussaint. Costello's third wife is jazz pianist Diana Krall. The man who kicked off Live Aid in 1985 with a knowing solo cover of The Beatles' 'All You Need Is Love' has arguably proved too diverse in his output to make an indelible mark on popular music. Yet his fans remain hugely loyal, and there's little doubt that his ability as a wordsmith is matched by few on the rock scene.

GENRES

Pub Rock, New Wave

ACTIVE YEARS

1977–present

CLASSIC RECORDINGS

My Aim Is True, This Year's Model, Armed Forces, 'Oliver's Army', Get Happy, Almost Blue

CREAM

VOCAL/INSTRUMENTAL GROUP

The first and arguably most famous of hard rock's much touted 'supergroups', Cream comprised Eric Clapton on guitar/vocals, Jack Bruce on bass/harmonica/keyboards/vocals and Ginger Baker on drums. The trio achieved lasting fame courtesy of their technical skills, jam-and-solo-laden concerts and four psychedelia-fuelled blues-rock albums. All this during the space of less than two and a half years and amidst incessant and wearying touring.

Cream's second album *Disraeli Gears* (1967) contained their most famous tracks 'Strange Brew', 'Tales Of Brave Ulysses' and 'Sunshine Of Your Love', but the group were in their element on stage, a fact only partly reflected in *Wheels Of Fire* (1968). This was a studio-and-stage two-album set that contained both the band's worst excesses and some of its finest moments, not least Jack Bruce's superb 'White Room' and the covers of Robert Johnson's 'Crossroads' and Albert King's 'Born Under A Bad Sign'. They split after 30 eventful months together. Clapton and Baker briefly reconvened in Blind Faith with Steve Winwood and a brief Cream reunion occurred in 2005 with concerts in London and New York, the highlights released on CD/DVD.

GENRES

Blues Rock, Hard Rock, Psychedelic Rock

ACTIVE YEARS

1966–68, 2005

CLASSIC RECORDINGS

Fresh Cream, 'I Feel Free', *Disraeli Gears*, 'Strange Brew', 'Sunshine Of Your Love', *Wheels Of Fire*, 'White Room', *Goodbye*

CREEDENCE CLEARWATER REVIVAL
VOCAL/INSTRUMENTAL GROUP

If John Fogerty (vocals, guitar), Tom Fogerty (guitar), Stuart Cook (bass) and Doug Clifford (drums) were Californian hippy in appearance, their music harked back to the energy and stylistic clichés of 1950s rock'n'roll, and their spiritual home seemed to be the swamplands of the Deep South, as demonstrated in titles like 'Born On The Bayou' (1969). After 1969's 'Proud Mary' all but topped the US chart, they reached a global audience with 'Bad Moon Rising' reaching No. 1 in Australia and Britain, and comparable figures for the likes of 'Green River', 'Down On The Corner', 'Travelin' Band' and 'Up Around The Bend'. Their albums appealed to heavy rock and mainstream pop fans alike.

The winning streak came to an end in 1972. Following the band's split, chief among composer John Fogerty's solo hits was 1975's 'Rockin' All Over The World' – adopted as a signature tune by Status Quo. It remains a mystery why Fogerty took a decade out of the music business from 1986–97 having topped the US chart a couple of years previously with the *Centerfield* (1985) album. He seemed more comfortable being a cult artist, and that is what he remains to this day – albeit one with an enviable back catalogue.

GENRES
Rock'n'Roll, Swamp Rock, Southern Rock

ACTIVE YEARS
1967–72

CLASSIC RECORDINGS
'Proud Mary', 'Bad Moon Rising', 'Green River', 'Down On The Corner', *Cosmo's Factory*, 'Travelin' Band', 'Up Around The Bend'

CROSBY, STILLS & NASH
VOCAL/INSTRUMENTAL GROUP

When on a US tour with The Hollies, Graham Nash (vocals, guitar) had sown the seeds of a 'supergroup' with ex–Byrd Dave Crosby (vocals, guitar) and Steve Stills (vocals, guitar) from Buffalo Springfield. The new group rehearsed in London for a 1969 eponymous album that featured hippy lyricism, flawless vocal harmonies and neo–acoustic backing tracks. Its spin-off single, Nash's 'Marrakesh Express', was a worldwide smash, and, while his trio's warblings were not to everyone's taste, they were well received at Woodstock – only their second stage appearance. They were joined on stage by Neil Young, a Buffalo Springfield colleague of Stills, who stayed on for 1970's *Deja Vu*, attributed to Crosby, Stills, Nash & Young. The group broke up the following year to devote themselves principally to solo careers, though the four individuals reunited for Live Aid and a 1988 album, *American Dream*.

Crosby, Stills & Nash celebrated the fortieth anniversary of *Deja Vu* with what had now become an annual world tour. They celebrated their survival – Crosby from crack cocaine and Stills from prostate cancer – by showing their harmonies had survived both the trials and the passing years: an album of classic covers from their contemporaries' songbooks was eagerly awaited by fans. No longer changing the world, but still entertaining it.

GENRES
Folk Rock

ACTIVE YEARS
1968–70, 1974, 1977–present

CLASSIC RECORDINGS
Crosby, Stills & Nash, 'Marrakesh Express', *Déjà Vu*, 'Woodstock', 'Ohio', *4 Way Street*, *So Far*, *CSN*, 'Just A Song Before I Go'

DEF LEPPARD
VOCAL/INSTRUMENTAL GROUP

Def Leppard appropriately formed in Sheffield, erstwhile home of the British steel industry. Their fresh brand of poppy heavy metal, led by Joe Elliott (vocals) and Pete Willis (lead guitar), soon won them fans. An early B-side 'Hello America' hinted at their ambitions. Debut album *On Through The Night* (1980) just missed the US Top 50; but with 1983's *Pyromania* they became giants of the genre, hitting the stateside chart at No. 2. Drummer Rick Allen lost an arm in a car accident, but adapted his kit, and 1987's *Hysteria* made the US No. 1 and UK No. 2. Guitarist Steve Clark died from drink and drugs in 1991, but once again the band returned, topping the charts with *Adrenalize* (1992).

Since these heady days – replete with smashes such as 'Love Bites' and 'Let's Get Rocked' – they have modernized successfully on *Slang* (1996), *Euphoria* (1999) and *X* (2002). Their pioneering, catchy, pop rock still draws crowds. The current line-up with Viv Campbell and Phil Collen on guitars with bassist Rick Savage, Elliot and Allen is now the longest lasting. A 2008 album of covers, entitled *Songs From The Sparkle Lounge*, debuted at No. 5 in the US, suggesting they still had life in them yet – though in 2010 they announced a hiatus.

GENRES
Hard Rock, Heavy Metal

ACTIVE YEARS
1977–present

CLASSIC RECORDINGS
Pyromania, *Hysteria*, 'Love Bites', *Adrenalize*, 'Let's Get Rocked', *Slang*, *Euphoria*, *X*, *Songs From The Sparkle Lounge*

BO DIDDLEY

GUITAR, VOCALS

Born Ellas Bates in McComb, Mississippi, Bo Diddley developed his guitar skills and stage persona in Chicago. He had his first guitar by the age of 10. By 1951, aged 23, he was a regular in clubs on Chicago's South Side. By 1955 he was signed to Checker, a spinoff of Chess Records. His debut single was a two-sided gem that featured his compositions 'Bo Diddley' and 'I'm A Man'. This single gave the world the 'Bo Diddley beat', a staccato rhythm that was picked up and used in hits by Buddy Holly ('Not Fade Away') and The Who ('Magic Bus'), among others. Diddley was also known for his 'cigar box' guitar, which he first designed and built in 1945 while in school. Songs such as 'You Don't Love Me', 'Pretty Thing', 'Diddy Wah Diddy', 'Who Do You Love?' and 'Mona' reflect the energy and drive of early rock'n'roll.

Many bands scored hits with Bo Diddley songs, and he was bitter at those who'd profited from his pioneering work – 'I opened the door for a lot of people, and they just ran through and left me holding the knob,' he told *The New York Times*. But The Clash paid him back in 1979 when they booked him as their opening act, a star-struck Joe Strummer admitting, 'I can't look at him without my mouth falling open.'

GENRES

Rock'n'Roll, R&B, Blues, Funk

ACTIVE YEARS

1951–2008

CLASSIC RECORDINGS

'Bo Diddley'/'I'm A Man', 'You Don't Love Me', 'Pretty Thing', 'Diddy Wah Diddy', 'Who Do You Love?', 'Mona'

DiRE STRAiTS

VOCAL/iNSTRUMENTAL GROUP

Led by guitarist and vocalist Mark Knopfler with brother David (vocals, guitar), John Illsley (bass) and Pick Withers (drums), Dire Straits went from playing the London pub circuit to a US hit album. Mark's inventive, plectrum-free guitar playing, street-poet lyrics and fine pop-rock songwriting combined to launch their huge career. Debut single, 'Sultans Of Swing', was a punchy, likeable helping of Dylanesque roots rock. *Communique* (1979) and *Love Over Gold* (1982) paved the way for the multiple-platinum *Brothers In Arms* (1985). 'Money For Nothing' from the latter satirized the very business they were in.

Only one studio album, 1991's slightly disappointing *On Every Street*, followed, and Mark Knopfler has since been linked with such talents as Emmylou Harris, Chet Atkins and James Taylor in pursuing a solo career that included soundtrack composition. The highlights of his concerts, however, remained the lite numbers of Dire Straits anthems he deigned to include. One early venture, 1990's Notting Hillbillies country guitar trio with Brendan Croker and Steve Phillips, overlapped Dire Straits and gave Knopfler a UK No. 2 album – his non-Straits peak to date. Dire Straits will be remembered as an intelligent but accessible band that could run the gamut from the borderline experimental (the intro to 1982's 'Private Investigations') to the chug-a-long pop rock of 'Walk Of Life' (1985).

GENRES

Rock

ACTIVE YEARS

1977–95

CLASSIC RECORDiNGS

Dire Straits, 'Sultans Of Swing', *Communiqué*, *Love Over Gold*, *Brothers In Arms*, 'Money For Nothing', 'Walk Of Life', *On Every Street*

THE DOORS

VOCAL/INSTRUMENTAL GROUP

The Doors were the antidote to the Love Generation – prototype punks who wrote their own musical manifesto. In Jim Morrison, the leather–clad Lizard King, they had rock's ultimate dark, Satanic anti–hero. Their active career was relatively brief – less than four and a half years from their chart debut until the death of their most unique selling point, Morrison. Yet The Doors packed a lot of controversy into that time, as well as a series of timeless and unforgettable records.

Morrison (vocals) has been the posthumous subject of a movie that fuelled the myth that he *was* The Doors. While his stage antics brought the Los Angeles outfit much publicity – and notoriety – their hits were either team efforts or written by other personnel, namely Ray Manzarek (keyboards), Robbie Krieger (guitar) and John Densmore (drums). Manzarek and Morrison had been fellow UCLA film students, choosing the name either from a poem by William Blake – 'If the doors of perception were cleansed, man could see things as they truly are: infinite' – or Aldous Huxley's *The Doors Of Perception*, a description of the results of the use of the drug mescaline.

EARLY CHART SUCCESS

The Doors were discovered after playing a residency at Los Angeles' legendary Whisky A Go Go club. Unlike their New York counterparts The Velvet Underground, whose bleak, apocalyptic view of life they shared, The Doors seemed unable to put a foot wrong commercially. 'Light My Fire', a US No. 1 in 1967, was followed by further high placings in both the single and album lists, peaking in 1968 with million–sellers 'Hello, I Love You' and 'Touch Me'. An eponymous debut album (1967) peaked at US No. 2 and contained 'The End', a lengthy track whose sensational lyric included a section where Morrison describes going into his parents' bedroom and tells his father he wants to kill him and his mother that he wants to seduce her.

TOP 100
ROCK ARTISTS

Subsequent albums like *Strange Days* (1967, with the extended 'When The Music's Over' rivalling 'The End'), *Morrison Hotel* (1970) and *L.A. Woman* (1971) all contained their share of classics, with Manzarek's organ and keyboard bass (the quartet had no regular bass player) prominent alongside Krieger's stabbing, bittersweet guitar. But with the first five of their six albums being released in three years, it was astounding that the musical quality held up as well as it did. There were relatively few bad tracks, though the middle two albums – *Waiting For The Sun* (1968) and *The Soft Parade* (1969) – were weakest in songwriting terms.

THE CURSE OF SUCCESS

Then came a concert in Miami where Morrison was purported to have exposed himself. During a long wait for the scheduled trial, Morris moved to Paris. Convicted and sentenced to six months in jail, Morrison died suddenly while still in Paris in 1971. Doors producer Paul Rothchild believed him to be 'a haunted man'. He was cursed by his own brilliance. He definitely had that poet's curse. He rode with madness. That was what chased him his whole life. He both explored it and fled from it.'

The Doors continued without Morrison and produced two further albums before disbanding. They reconvened in 1978 to provide accompaniment on *An American Prayer*, an album centred on tapes of Morrison reciting self-written poems. Since then, Manzarek and Krieger have toured with a new lead singer, The Cult's Ian Astbury, much to Densmore's legally expressed disapproval.

GENRES

Psychedelic Rock, Hard Rock

ACTIVE YEARS

1965–73

CLASSIC RECORDINGS

The Doors, 'Light My Fire', *Waiting For The Sun*, 'Hello, I Love You', 'Touch Me', *Morrison Hotel*, *L.A. Woman*

BOB DYLAN

GUITAR, HARMONICA, SINGER/SONGWRITER

Bob Dylan was the most influential solo artist of his generation. Writing and performing songs, his poetic, sometimes-abstract, often-philosophical lyrics spoke to the masses during an era of social unrest, political upheaval and radical change. While cross-pollinating folk and country with electric rock, Dylan elevated the role of the singer/songwriter and subsequently introduced an entirely new dimension to popular music.

FROM ZIMMERMAN TO DYLAN

Born Robert Allen Zimmerman in Duluth, Minnesota, and raised in nearby Hibbing, the future icon learned to play guitar and harmonica as a child while influenced by radio broadcasts of country, blues and, during his mid-teens, rock'n'roll. This led to his participation in several high-school rock bands. While studying art at the University of Minnesota in Minneapolis, a burgeoning interest in American folk music prompted Zimmerman to take the name of Welsh poet Dylan Thomas and, as Bob Dylan, he performed on the local folk music circuit. (He would legally change his name in August 1962.)

Having quit college at the end of his freshman year to become a full-time musician, Dylan was returning from Chicago to Minneapolis in January 1961 when he decided to head for New York City instead. That April, Dylan opened for bluesman John Lee Hooker at Gerde's Folk City, and on the strength of a *New York Times* review of a later gig, A&R exec John Hammond signed Dylan to Columbia Records and produced his eponymous first album. *Bob Dylan*, released in March 1962, reflected Dylan's live repertoire, with just a couple of original compositions among an assortment of folk, blues and gospel standards. It was a different story by the time *The Freewheelin' Bob Dylan* was released in May 1963, a cover of 'Corrine, Corrina' standing alone amid a dozen self-penned tracks. Given the political climate, two songs attracted the most attention, 'A Hard Rain's A-Gonna Fall' conjured brutal images of nuclear Armageddon while 'Blowin' In The Wind', with its heartfelt call for change, became an international chart-topper in the summer of 1963 for Peter, Paul & Mary.

Dylan's more conventional pop renditions helped broaden his appeal. He embarked on a relationship with the reigning Queen of Folk, Joan Baez, who recorded several of his songs. Successful covers were also recorded during the next few years by the likes of The Hollies, Herman's Hermits, Judy Collins, Sonny & Cher, Manfred Mann, The Turtles and, most famously, The Byrds. Meanwhile, Dylan's songwriting was advancing at a rapid rate. The January 1964 release of *The Times They Are A-Changin'* continued the cycle of protest songs in its outstanding title track. Yet, just eight months later, *Another Side Of Bob Dylan* proved to be just that; partly more romantic, invariably more poetic, with greater depth and imagery to classics like 'All I Really Want To Do', 'Chimes Of Freedom', 'My Back Pages' and 'It Ain't Me Babe'.

BROADENED APPEAL

Dylan now opted to explore the much broader possibilities of electric folk rock. *Bringing It All Back Home*, released in March 1965, projected him into the pop mainstream, its first side featuring a heavily amplified five-piece band on numbers like 'Maggie's Farm' and 'Subterranean Homesick Blues', with its Chuck Berry-type melody and repetitive, bridge-less arrangement. 'Mr Tambourine Man' appeared on the all-acoustic second side of the record, alongside gems like 'It's Alright, Ma (I'm Only Bleeding)' and 'It's All Over Now, Baby Blue'. These tracks revealed their composer eschewing social commentary in favour of personal expression. Dylan rammed home his message that summer at the Newport Folk Festival, where his electrified performance with members of The Paul Butterfield Blues Band drew boos from many in the crowd. Still, by then he'd secured a massive worldwide audience with breakthrough single 'Like A Rolling Stone', which peaked at No. 2 on the US charts and, at just over six minutes, was twice the length of conventional releases. Dylan was redefining the parameters of popular music. 'Like A Rolling Stone' was the curtain raiser to August 1965's *Highway 61 Revisited*. Dylan was now a streetwise beat poet, and this reached its apotheosis on arguably his finest record, the double album *Blonde On Blonde* (1966).

Supported in the studio as on the road by rockabilly singer Ronnie Hawkins' former backing group The Hawks (renamed The Band a couple of years later), Dylan wove a texture that combined his favourite musical genres – folk, rock, country and blues – with surreal imagery and witty wordplay. Yet there was also a tender beauty to songs like 'Visions Of Johanna', 'I Want You', 'Just Like A Woman' and 'Sad Eyed Lady Of The Lowlands'.

On 29 July 1966, just over two months after *Blonde On Blonde*'s release, Dylan suffered a near-fatal motorcycle accident near his home in Woodstock, New York, and became a changed man. The *John Wesley Harding* (1967) and *Nashville Skyline* (1969) albums signalled Dylan's foray into the much calmer waters of country rock. The latter even spawned a Top 10 single in the form of 'Lay Lady Lay'.

NEW DIRECTIONS

Although 1970's *Self Portrait* incited the first uniformly critical drubbing of Dylan's career, the new decade saw him sustain a fairly high degree of success (if not as much influence) with the albums *New Morning* (1970), *Planet Waves* (1974), *Blood On The Tracks* (1975), *Desire* (1976), *Street Legal* (1978) and *Slow Train Coming* (1979). The last record followed on the heels of his conversion from Judaism to Christianity, yet two subsequent born-again projects were met with derision and thereafter the Jewish re-convert made the artistically wise decision to keep religion out of his music.

Since 1988, Dylan has fronted what has come to be known as his 'Never Ending Tour' of the globe, while returning to form in the studio. *Together Through Life*, his first studio album since 2006, hit the top slot on both sides of the Atlantic in 2009, making him the oldest living person to go straight into the chart at No. 1. He remains one of the world's most formidable and relevant artists.

GENRES

Folk, Blues, Gospel, Folk Rock, Country

ACTIVE YEARS

1961–present

CLASSIC RECORDINGS

The Freewheelin' Bob Dylan, Bringing It All Back Home, Blonde On Blonde, Nashville Skyline, Blood On The Tracks, Desire, Modern Times

THE EAGLES

VOCAL/INSTRUMENTAL GROUP

The Eagles defined the sound of California in the 1970s and were its most successful exponents. The band formed out of the Los Angeles country rock scene in 1970, when guitarist Glenn Frey, drummer Don Henley, guitarist Bernie Leadon and bassist Randy Meisner were recruited as Linda Ronstadt's group for her *Silk Purse* album.

The experienced quartet came to London to record their debut album, *The Eagles* (1972), with producer Glyn Johns (The Rolling Stones, The Who, Steve Miller). They combined the country rock of The Byrds and The Flying Burrito Brothers with a harder sound and carefully arranged harmonies. *The Eagles* went gold in America, spawning three hit singles: 'Witchy Woman', 'Take It Easy' (written by Frey with Jackson Browne) and 'Peaceful Easy Feeling'.

They returned to London for *Desperado* (1973), a conceptual album that drew parallels with cowboy culture and the rock'n'roll lifestyle. It was less successful than their debut, although 'Tequila Sunrise' became one of their most popular songs. For *On The Border* (1974) The Eagles switched to Los Angeles and producer Bill Szymczyk (who would produce their subsequent albums), adding guitarist Don Felder to the line-up. Their slicker sound brought them their first US No. 1 with 'Best Of My Love'. *One Of These Nights* (1975) topped the US charts for five weeks and included three big hits – 'One Of These Nights', 'Lyin' Eyes' and 'Take It To The Limit' – that all charted in the UK along with the album.

TROUBLE AT THE TOP

Hotel California (1976) was The Eagles' pinnacle. Painstakingly recorded, it caught the full decadence of their vision of the American dream in a blaze of guitars, acerbic lyrics and tight harmonies. It was No. 1 in America for eight weeks, produced two No. 1 singles – 'New Kid In Town' and the title track – and won five Grammy Awards.

Meanwhile, The Eagles' increasingly commercial style, spiralling success and internal tensions caused Leadon to leave in 1976. He was replaced by guitarist Joe Walsh, who was previously in The James Gang and had released several solo albums. Meisner, too, bailed out in late 1977. His replacement was bassist Timothy B. Schmit who had followed Meisner into Poco. But it was another two years before The Eagles completed their next album as their obsessive quest for perfection and strained relations hampered their creativity. *The Long Run* (1979) continued to break the band's own records, spending nine weeks at No. 1 and featuring three more major hits: 'Heartache Tonight', 'The Long Run' and 'I Can't Tell You Why'. By the time *Live* (1980) came out the band had broken up. However, the split was not made official until 1982.

WHEN HELL FREEZES OVER

The group members spent the next decade pursuing solo careers. Whenever Henley was asked when The Eagles would reform he replied, 'when Hell freezes over'. The album of that name (1994) was the result of two years inching towards a reunion. There were four new songs plus tracks from the MTV concert that launched their comeback. Since then they have toured periodically, sacked Don Felder and recorded the all-new *Long Road Out Of Eden* (2007). Meanwhile *Eagles: Their Greatest Hits 1971–75* (1975) continues to sell and has already sold over 28 million copies.

GENRES

Country Rock, Folk Rock

ACTIVE YEARS

1970–80, 1994–present

CLASSIC RECORDINGS

'Best Of My Love', *One Of These Nights*, *Hotel California*, 'New Kid In Town', 'Hotel California', *The Long Run*, *Long Road Out Of Eden*

EMINEM

RAPPER

Marshall Bruce Mathers III was born in Detroit, Michigan, his upbringing reputedly poverty-stricken. At an early age, Mathers entered the hip-hop world with gusto. Taking the name Eminem (after his initials), he performed from the age of 13. The 2002 film *8 Mile* (named after an area of Detroit), in which Eminem played himself, explores his early career.

Eminem's *Slim Shady LP* (1999) revealed the a damaged side of the rapper. The album sold triple platinum in its first year and *The Marshall Mathers LP* (2000) sold three times as well. Later albums were perhaps too infused with Mathers' increasing mental instability to cross over as well as previously. Eminem diversified his talents, producing other artists and guesting in the group D-12. However, his career ran out of steam after 2004's *Encore*. He published the 2008 autobiography *The Way I Am* and returned to the musical fray in 2009 with *Relapse*. While this album didn't manage to sell as well as previous efforts (some five million worldwide), it was named one of the top albums of the year.

GENRES

Hip Hop

ACTIVE YEARS

1995–present

CLASSIC RECORDINGS

The Slim Shady LP, 'My Name Is', *The Marshall Mathers LP*, 'Stan', *Music From 8 Mile*, 'Lose Yourself', *Encore*, *Relapse*

FLEETWOOD MAC
VOCAL/INSTRUMENTAL GROUP

Peter Green (born Peter Greenbaum, vocals, guitar) had been a star of John Mayall's Bluesbreakers in which John McVie (bass) and Mick Fleetwood (drums) had toiled less visibly in the rhythm section. On leaving Mayall in 1967, the three became 'Peter Green's Fleetwood Mac' after enlisting guitarist Jeremy Spencer. Later, a third guitarist, Danny Kirwan, was added. The outfit began moving away from its blues core with hits penned by Green.

The first incarnation of the band was one of Britain's biggest late-1960s attractions. Green's talents were considered comparable to Eric Clapton. Santana covered 'Black Magic Woman', while Jeremy Spencer, who didn't always play on the records, was a consummate showman who covered Green's lack of on-stage confidence. However, Green's exit after a bad drugs trip and that of Spencer, who joined a religious sect, in 1970 brought the group to its knees. The enlistment of McVie's wife, Christine Perfect (vocals, keyboards) from Chicken Shack papered over the cracks but more upheavals preceded a relocation to California in the mid-1970s. New American recruits Lindsey Buckingham (guitar, vocals) and Stevie Nicks (vocals) looked as good as they sounded and gave the band a much-needed boost. Albums *Fleetwood Mac* (1975) and *Rumours* (1977) were both US chart-toppers, the latter also No. 1 in UK, their polished studio sound making them radio favourites. Hit singles like 'Dreams', 'Don't Stop' and 'Rhiannon' boosted sales.

HEARTACHE AND HITS

Buckingham and Nicks had been a couple when they joined the band but their romance quickly hit the rocks. The McVies also split, Christine romancing the lighting engineer. Affairs by (and sometimes between) band members and their subsequent repercussions proved the inspiration for songs like 'Go Your Own Way', 'I Don't Want To Know' and 'Never Going Back Again'.

Fleetwood Mac's music welded the rock-solid rhythmic foundation of Mick Fleetwood and John McVie to a sunshine West Coast sound overlaid with the contrasting dual female vocals of Nicks (sensual, breathy) and Christine McVie (bluesy and honest). With the addition of Buckingham's imploring tenor and songwriting skills, it was the recipe for success of Eagles-like proportions. Double album *Tusk* (1979) was disappointing and overblown, however, and a mid-1980s hiatus ensued until 1987's UK chart-topping *Tango In The Night* brought the band back to the spotlight.

MAC MARK ii

In 1988, session guitarist Rick Vito (Bob Seger, John Mayall) and singer Billy Burnette, son of rockabilly legend Johnny, replaced Buckingham for *Behind The Mask*. But when that album only made No. 18 in the US (but No. 1 in the UK), and Stevie Nicks and Christine McVie handed in their notice, it was clear only the classic *Rumours* line-up would do for US fans. Sure enough, Mac Mark II put their many differences aside and reformed in 1997, and their first new studio album since 1987, *Say You Will* (2003), proved there was life in them yet. Prior to that, they had played at Bill Clinton's Presidential inauguration in 1993, the song 'Don't Stop' having served as his election anthem.

At the same time, after many years in the wilderness, Peter Green managed a comeback in the 1990s, recording *Splinter Group* (1997) with the identically named backing band and enjoying a low-key career renaissance thereafter. His early creations like UK instrumental chart-topper 'Albatross', 'Oh Well', 'Man Of The World' and 'Green Manalishi' had however weathered the passage of time better than the glossy hits of the second incarnation.

GENRES

Blues Rock, Rock, Pop

ACTIVE YEARS

1967–present

CLASSIC RECORDINGS

Mr Wonderful, 'Albatross', 'Oh Well', *Fleetwood Mac*, *Rumours*, 'Dreams', *Tusk*, *Mirage*, *Tango In The Night*

TOP 100
ROCK ARTISTS

FOO FIGHTERS
VOCAL/INSTRUMENTAL GROUP

Foo Fighters, the post–Nirvana band of Dave Grohl, with Taylor Hawkins (drums), Nate Mendel (bass) and Chris Shiflett (guitar), saw the drummer turned singer storm the charts again and again with an honest, workaday approach to rock that was, more often that not, humorously handled. Thankfully, Grohl could write a melody, which ensured his new band made countless radio hits. Singles such as 'This Is A Call', 'I'll Stick Around' (both 1995), 'My Hero', 'Walking After You' (both 1997) were all more radio–friendly than the last. Often the singles would come backed with hammy promotional films, but while critics accused Grohl of selling out, the likeable singer and the quality of his songwriting won through.

The acoustic tour that took place in the summer of 2006 featured an augmented line–up echoing Nirvana's MTV Unplugged phase. The set list focused on the acoustic half of recent double album *In Your Honour* (2005). While the Foos were playing the largest venues of their career, including New York's Madison Square Garden, former workaholic Grohl was to become a father of two in 2009 and understandably craved a home life with second wife Jordyn. The band duly released a *Greatest Hits* in 2009, then took a break as Grohl played with supergroup Them Crooked Vultures.

GENRES
Alternative Rock, Post–grunge

ACTIVE YEARS
1995–present

CLASSIC RECORDINGS
Foo Fighters, *The Colour And The Shape*, *One By One*, 'All My Life', *In Your Honour*, 'Best Of You', *Echoes, Silence, Patience & Grace*

ARETHA FRANKLIN

VOCALS

Since the title was first applied to her in the late 1960s, Aretha Franklin has been hailed as the undisputed Queen of Soul. Possessing a voice of power and passion (and underrated skills on the piano), she has turned her attention to everything from pop through jazz to classical. With a grounding in gospel, however, it was in soul music that she found her finest hours and her true home.

Aretha was born in Memphis, Tennessee, to parents who were both nationally successful singers. She moved to Detroit with her family in 1949 and made her first recordings at the age of 14, singing hymns in her father's New Bethel Baptist Church. She also toured with her father and sisters Carolyn and Erma (who would both go on to have successful singing careers of their own). By 1960, she was tackling secular material, and was signed by John Hammond to Columbia (it is rumoured she had also been wooed by Motown). Columbia saw her as a crossover pop and jazz artist and, although she had a string of minor hits for them in the early 1960s (the biggest a cover of the Al Jolson standard 'Rock–A–Bye Your Baby With A Dixie Melody'), her talent was generally not well served by the choice of material.

THE ATLANTIC YEARS

If the Columbia recordings were poorly judged, things came together perfectly when she moved to Atlantic Records. Legend has it that Louise Bishop, a Philadelphia disc jockey, called Aretha to advise her that Atlantic was interested in signing her. By January of 1967, she was in Muscle Shoals, Alabama, seated at the piano recording the first of 14 million–selling singles for the label.

The combination of Franklin and producer Jerry Wexler, arranger Arif Mardin and the rock–solid R&B of the Muscle Shoals rhythm section proved a winner. 'I Never Loved A Man (The Way I Love You)', opened her account at No. 9.

The hastily convened second single produced one of the defining moments of popular music, her blazing take on Otis Redding's 'Respect'. It was an instant US No. 1, resonating resoundingly with the rising confidence and pride of the black community.

The success of 'Respect' was instrumental in the introduction of a new Grammy Award category in 1967, that of Best Female R&B Vocal. Aretha won the accolade for the next eight years. From the start at Atlantic, and perhaps as the legacy of her Columbia years, she tackled material by an eclectic range of writers from both within the circle of soul and beyond: Goffin & King, Lennon & McCartney, Bacharach & David, Curtis Mayfield and Elton John all received early attention and chart success in her hands. With her gospel roots, Aretha was a gifted arranger of vocals on many of her hits, and she and her sister Carolyn also featured in writing credits.

Unusually for a female soul singer at that time, her albums also sold consistently well. Her domination of the charts continued in the early 1970s and included what many consider to be her finest LP, the 1972 live, double gospel set *Amazing Grace*. By the mid-1970s, however, she was beginning to lose her way; experimenting with different producers, the recordings (and the live concerts) became more lavish productions, but the choice of songs was erratic, with some ill-judged departures into disco.

THE LATER YEARS

A switch of labels to Arista in 1980 had little initial impact, although a cameo appearance in the film *The Blues Brothers* the same year helped to re-establish the reputation of her influential early work. The year 1985 saw a return to form: a UK Top 10 entry with the anthemic Eurythmics collaboration 'Sisters Are Doin' It For Themselves', and a US No. 1 with 'Freeway Of Love'. Her rousing 1986 duet with George Michael 'I Knew You Were Waiting' was No. 1 in both the UK and US.

Aretha notched up 89 Top 40 entries on the R&B chart between 1960 and 1992, 17 of which reached the top spot. She was the first black woman to appear on the cover of *Time* magazine, was the recipient of a Presidential Medal Of Honor and owns both a Grammy Lifetime Achievement Award and a Grammy Living Legend Award.

Last but not least, in 1987 she became the first woman to be inducted into the Rock And Roll Hall Of Fame. The reason for these awards and accolades is a voice with a four-octave range that, combined with peerless breath control, allows her, in the words of that historic *Time* magazine cover story from 1969, 'to spin out long phrases that curl sinuously around the beat and dangle tantalizingly from blue notes'.

A LIVING LEGEND

With more US pop and R&B hits than any other woman, Franklin's status as a soul institution is assured. But rather than see the century out with an untaxing schedule of celebrity duets and compilation releases, she drew admiration in 1998 for *A Rose Is Still A Rose*, on which she worked with contemporary R&B artists (notably on the Lauryn Hill title track). That same year she made an impromptu live performance at the Grammy Awards show where she sang Luciano Pavarotti's 'Nessun Dorma' when the opera star was indisposed. 'I'm a very versatile vocalist,' Aretha told *Time*. 'That's what I think a singer should be. Whatever it is, I can sing it.' Her autobiography, published in 1999, was entitled *From These Roots*. In 2006, aged 64, she won her seventeenth Grammy and performed 'My Country 'Tis Of Thee' at Barack Obama's presidential inauguration in 2009.

GENRES

Soul, Jazz, Rock, Pop, Blues, R&B, Gospel, Classical

ACTIVE YEARS

1956–present

CLASSIC RECORDINGS

I Never Loved A Man The Way I Love You, 'Respect', *Aretha Now*, *Young, Gifted And Black*, *Amazing Grace*, 'I Knew You Were Waiting (For Me)'

MARVIN GAYE

VOCALS

Gaye was a soul giant whose career spanned his genre's transition from pop entertainment to social conscience and personal exploration. He signed with Berry Gordy's Motown label in 1961, where his recordings revealed a strong tenor voice with a huge span – three octaves – on songs ranging from R&B mod anthem 'Can I Get A Witness' to the soulful heartache of 'I Heard It Through The Grapevine'. He enjoyed two separate careers at Motown, the first singing the words of others and the second as one of a new breed of singer, songwriter and performer. He paralleled the likes of Stevie Wonder and Curtis Mayfield, broadening soul's boundaries to reflect a changing world.

Marvin Pentz Gaye was born in Washington, the son of a church minister. Like so many he enjoyed his first musical education through the church, playing organ and singing in the choir, but was a rebellious spirit. At the age of 15, he joined doo-wop group The Rainbows, which also included Don Covay, before winning a talent contest with Harvey Fuqua's group The Moonglows. A spell in the United States Air Force, where early psychological problems may have manifested themselves, only briefly interrupted his career and in time both he and Fuqua ended up in Detroit. When the label Fuqua founded was absorbed into the new Tamla concern, Marvin earned money playing drums on sessions for The Miracles and Stevie Wonder.

A NATURAL TALENT

His ambitions, however, demanded more than a back seat on someone else's recordings and he was soon out front at the microphone. When The Rolling Stones covered one of his early US hits, 'Can I Get A Witness', on their first album, the name of Marvin Gaye became known to a hip white audience, too. The singer manufactured his own success with only his fourth solo release: 'Stubborn Kind Of Fellow' was to be the first of over 20 glorious hits for Tamla, where his natural talents were teamed with producers like Holland-Dozier-Holland, Norman Whitfield and Smokey Robinson.

His individual successes included 'Can I Get A Witness', 'Ain't That Peculiar' and 'How Sweet It Is To Be Loved By You'. In tandem with Kim Weston, 'It Takes Two' got the thumbs-up from his adoring public, as did 'Ain't No Mountain High Enough', 'Ain't Nothing Like The Real Thing', 'Your Precious Love' and 'You're All I Need To Get By', where the combination of Gaye and Tammi Terrell grabbed the public's imagination. These romantic duets with Weston and Terrell ran in parallel with his solo success.

In 1968 Gaye found himself at the top of the charts in both the UK and US with 'I Heard It Through The Grapevine' – a success despite Gladys Knight having already had a major US hit with the haunting Norman Whitfield song. But his memorable partnership with Tammi Terrell ended tragically in March 1970 when she died of a brain tumour. Gaye was inconsolable.

THE GREATEST SOUL ALBUM AND BEYOND

Terrell's death saw Gaye disappear for a year, then emerge to pull together the strands of his life and career. Like Stevie Wonder he would demand total artistic control of his output rather than working within the Motown writer/producer-led system. The results were astonishing. *What's Going On* (1971) is regarded as the greatest soul album ever and took a radical, mature new direction, addressing political and social issues like inner-city decay, Vietnam and pollution. Its follow-up *Let's Get It On* (1973) dealt equally powerfully with more intimate concerns. Whereas before Gaye's success had been singles-based, now it was his albums that were drawing great praise. That said, the title track of *Let's Get It On* gave him another US No. 1, while in the same year an album made with Diana Ross – *Diana & Marvin* – generated three singles that made the US Top 50.

Marvin had married Anna, sister of Motown boss Berry Gordy, so their break up inevitably precipitated trouble with the label. The 1978 album *Here My Dear* was so titled because its profits went to pay his divorce settlement. His musical output became patchy, though songs cut with Diana Ross were sizeable hits, and he acknowledged the disco boom with 'Got To Give It Up'. Sadly, something he could not give up was drugs, and under their influence he became ever more reclusive and bitter.

After leaving Motown having scored an American No. 1 in April 1977 with 'Got To Give It Up', he spent some time living in Europe where he made one last daring attempt to reignite his now smouldering career. Signed to CBS/Columbia, he produced a magnificent album in *Midnight Love* (1982) and its internationally successful single 'Sexual Healing' and toured the States in the wake of the album's success.

A TRAGIC END

Although his creative light never dimmed, his later life was blighted by tax issues, drug dependency and depression. Returning home to live with his mother who was unwell, he found himself arguing incessantly with his 70-year-old father. On the eve of his forty-fifth birthday Marvin Gaye was shot with a gun he had given to his father for safekeeping.

A troubled genius, Marvin Gaye nevertheless managed to touch many lives with his music. He also established soul traditions that everyone from Michael Jackson through to Teddy Pendergrass to Usher learnt from – the moves, the vocal mannerisms. Several books have been written in an attempt to dig deeper into this complex personality: for most, though, the music remains the message.

GENRES

R&B, Soul, Doo-Wop, Funk

ACTIVE YEARS

1958–84

CLASSIC RECORDINGS

'I Heard It Through The Grapevine', *What's Going On, Let's Get It On, I Want You, Midnight Love*, 'Sexual Healing'

GENESIS

VOCAL/INSTRUMENTAL GROUP

The core of Genesis – Peter Gabriel (vocals), Tony Banks (keyboards) and Mike Rutherford (bass) – met at the (fee-paying) Charterhouse public school in the mid-1960s. The man who discovered them was also an ex-pupil – singer/producer/ Svengali Jonathan King. Recently formed from an amalgamation of two school outfits, The Garden Wall and The Anon, the band didn't even have a name, so he christened them Genesis. Their debut, 1969's *From Genesis To Revelation*, was a concept album, the ambitious idea being to tell the story of the evolution of mankind in 13 songs.

After the album's failure, King encouraged them to continue, introducing them to Tony Stratton Smith who would become their manager and, eventually, record-company boss when he founded his Charisma label. The recruitment of Steve Hackett (guitar, replacing original member Anthony Phillips) and Phil Collins (drums) in 1970 completed the classic line-up. They recorded *Nursery Cryme* (1971) and *Foxtrot* (1972), albums whose complex songs characterized English progressive rock. Numbers like 'The Knife' (from 1970's *Trespass*), 'The Musical Box' and 'Supper's Ready' were long, complex and heavily instrumental. This style was accompanied by Gabriel's penchant for dressing up in outlandish costumes and prosthetic masks, and increased the sense of theatre.

A RELUCTANT FRONTMAN

Selling England By The Pound (1973) was their commercial breakthrough, a No. 3 in Britain and the first Top 100 entry in the US, thanks partly to the single 'I Know What I Like (In Your Wardrobe)'. But tensions between Gabriel and his colleagues following the ambitious concept album *The Lamb Lies Down On Broadway* (1974) saw him quit. He was replaced at the microphone by the slightly reluctant Collins stepping forward from his kit after six years. With Collins out front, the material became noticeably more direct, hit singles became the rule rather than the exception and Genesis's unlikely crossover into the mainstream began. Other progressive bands like Gentle Giant tried to emulate

this happy accident, but failed and were swallowed up by the impending punk wave. The first Collins–fronted album, *A Trick Of The Tail* (1976), became the band's biggest US success so far reaching No. 31. Genesis continued to prosper as a trio when Hackett departed after 1977's *Wind And Wuthering*, bringing in American Daryl Stuermer for live work. Drummers Bill Bruford and, later, Chester Thompson also augmented the band on stage to give Collins licence to roam.

CONTINUED SUCCESS

Albums *Duke* (1980) and *Abacab* (1981) topped the UK chart (Nos. 11 and 7 in the US, respectively) as did *Genesis* (1983) and *Invisible Touch* (1986), but the complex prog–rock that had enthralled sixth–formers and students alike was now behind them. Meanwhile Collins topped the UK charts worldwide with 1981's *Face Value* album, kicking off a parallel solo career that more than equalled Genesis in success.

In the 1980s and 1990s, a more radio–friendly approach yielded the band's most commercially successful period, hits like 'I Can't Dance' from the UK chart–topping *We Can't Dance* (1991) introducing them to the MTV generation via self–deprecating videos. But in 1997 Collins left to concentrate on his solo career and Genesis made one more album – *Calling All Stations*, Genesis's first new studio album since 1991 – with their third lead singer Ray Wilson, formerly of Stiltskin. Genesis's period as a street–credible band ended with Peter Gabriel's departure, and Rutherford felt their new young singer could restore some of the edge lost as Phil Collins veered more towards the middle of the road. But the public did not agree. Somewhat inevitably, Collins, Rutherford and Banks reunited for live work in 2007.

GENRES

Progressive Rock, Rock, Pop

ACTIVE YEARS

1967–99, 2007–present

CLASSIC RECORDINGS

The Lamb Lies Down On Broadway, A Trick Of The Tail, Duke, Abacab, Genesis, Invisible Touch, 'Invisible Touch', We Can't Dance

THE GRATEFUL DEAD

VOCAL/INSTRUMENTAL GROUP

Rock's most famous and celebrated hippy band is known more for its anything-goes, drug-hazed concerts and legions of 'Deadhead' fans than for its body of studio work. The Grateful Dead grew out of a union between singer/songwriter/lead guitarist Jerry Garcia, songwriter/rhythm guitarist Bob Weir and keyboardist/singer Ron 'Pigpen' McKernan. They were to become the poster boys of the psychedelic scene that flourished in San Francisco during the mid- to late 1960s.

Garcia had played banjo in a number of bluegrass and jug bands when, in 1964, he first teamed up with blues/gospel enthusiast McKernan to form Mother McCree's Uptown Jug Champions, recruiting folk devotee Weir and several other musicians along the way. McKernan then persuaded Garcia and Weir to go electric, and it was as the amplified Warlocks that, in July 1965, they began performing around the Bay Area with classically trained avant-garde/electronica graduate Phil Lesh on bass and Bill Kreutzmann on drums.

Others to get on board included rock-solid second drummer Mickey Hart and avant-garde second keyboard player Tom Constanten. Equally important was a non-performing member, poet Robert Hunter, whose suitably abstract lyrics fitted the Garcia-penned, hallucinogen-fuelled songs.

UNIQUE AND ECLECTIC

It was not until the 1969 in-concert double-album *Live/Dead* was released that record buyers finally got to hear what the group was truly all about. Here were the free-form improvisational skills of the musicians in their unexpurgated, virtuosic glory. Back in the studio, the band recorded two classic albums in 1970 that represented a drastic change of pace and direction, contrasting sharply with its onstage act. Both the all-acoustic *Workingman's Dead* and the seminal *American Beauty* saw the Dead exploring their country, folk and blues roots.

TOP 100
ROCK ARTISTS

Live work would gather momentum with each passing year, but band members suffered the effects of substance abuse. McKernan's chronic alcoholism resulted in his death from liver failure at the age of 26, and Garcia had begun a battle with drug addiction. Pigpen's replacement Keith Godchaux and singer wife Donna's substance abuse would lead to their dismissal in 1979, a year before Keith's death in a car accident. Keith's replacement, Brent Mydland, would be around for just over a decade before he died from a drug overdose in 1990.

Wake Of The Flood (1973), *Grateful Dead From The Mars Hotel* (1974) and 1975's *Blues For Allah* albums, all released on the band's own label, were their last decent records for more than a decade. The touring continued, however, the band even playing at the foot of the pyramids in Egypt. Meanwhile, The band's various logos proved profitable as Deadheads grew up but wanted to maintain their allegiance and recall their nonconformist past via tie-dye T-shirts, car stickers, etc.

A RETURN TO FORM

The Dead's cult popularity went mainstream in 1987 courtesy of the band's highest-selling album, *In The Dark*. The album's success also spawned the band's only-ever Top 10 single, 'Touch Of Gray'. But Garcia's 1995 death from a heart attack while attending a drug abuse treatment centre in Northern California effectively ended The Grateful Dead story. The remaining members have continued to tour in different combinations, under the names The Other Ones and, latterly, The Dead. But, The Grateful Dead as it was originally will be remembered for inspiring a generation (or two) of jam bands. They were also notable in providing 'taper sections' at their venues for people who wanted to record the performance thus making music freely available long before file sharing.

GENRES

Rock, Bluegrass, Folk, Blues, Country, Jazz, Psychedelia

ACTIVE YEARS

1965–95

CLASSIC RECORDINGS

Anthem Of The Sun, Aoxomoxoa, Live/Dead, Workingman's Dead, American Beauty, From The Mars Hotel, In The Dark

GREEN DAY
VOCAL/INSTRUMENTAL GROUP

Californian rock trio Billie Joe Armstrong (vocals, guitar), Mike Dirnt (bass, vocals) and Tré Cool (drums) enjoyed global success with 1993's *Dookie*, their first album for a major label. They were Green Day – unashamed punk-rock throwbacks who made entertaining music videos.

The band turned to producing more carefully crafted pop fare but despite the odd flash of inspiration they could not recapture their early popularity. The highlight was 1997's *Nimrod*, which contained the acoustic gem 'Good Riddance (Time Of Your Life)' and featured just Armstrong and an acoustic guitar backed by cello. Then 2004's *American Idiot* hit a nerve by lampooning George W. Bush's America. It pushed them even higher up the rock ladder than before, and they proved more significant in directing the youth of the world's largest nation toward political opinion than any amount of governmental campaigning or advertising. They were in no hurry to follow it up, though a deluxe live album and DVD package, provocatively titled *Bullet In A Bible* (2005), helped meet demand. A musical based on the rock opera album *American Idiot* and directed by Michael Mayer hit Broadway in 2010. Green Day are now seen as innovators, and not the scene-hogging bandwagon-jumpers of the late 1980s many assumed they would be remembered as.

GENRES

Punk Rock, Pop

ACTIVE YEARS

1987–present

CLASSIC RECORDINGS

Dookie, *Nimrod*, 'Good Riddance (Time Of Your Life)', *Warning*, *American Idiot*, 'Boulevard Of Broken Dreams', *21st Century Breakdown*

GUNS N'ROSES

VOCAL/INSTRUMENTAL GROUP

Axl Rose (born William Bailey, vocals) and Izzy Stradlin (born Jeffrey Isbell, guitar) were joined by Slash (born Saul Hudson, guitar), Duff McKagan (bass) and Steve Adler (drums) to form a band that gave the heavy rock scene a mighty shaking. Signed to Geffen – after the 1986 EP *Live ?1*@ Like A Suicide* had attracted industry interest – their debut album *Appetite For Destruction* (1987) combined the attack of AC/DC with a punk aesthetic and powerful lyrics about the underbelly of L.A. It went to the US No. 1 spot, as did 'Sweet Child O' Mine'.

The next few years saw much debauchery; the departure of Adler; the US Top 5 ballad 'Patience'; and the releases of the massive-selling *Use Your Illusion I* and *II* (1991). Stradlin also jumped ship as, in 1995, did Slash, to form Slash's Snakepit and then Velvet Revolver. This left Rose attempting to keep the name of the band alive. Headlines, however, focused on no-shows, tantrums and delays to *Chinese Democracy* (2008), their sixth studio album and the first original since 1993. In May 2010, the album had sold only five million copies worldwide compared with *Appetite For Destruction*'s 28 million. Rose's reaction: he sued his manager....

GENRES

Hard Rock, Heavy Metal

ACTIVE YEARS

1985–present

CLASSIC RECORDINGS

Appetite For Destruction, 'Sweet Child O' Mine', *GN'R Lies*, 'Patience', *Use Your Illusion I and II*, 'November Rain', *Chinese Democracy*

BILL HALEY
GUITAR, VOCALS

William John Clifton Haley was born in Highland Park, Detroit, and raised near Chester, Pennsylvania. In his late teens he joined a working country and western band, The Downhomers, later forming The Saddlemen. In 1952, they became Bill Haley & His Comets. 'Crazy Man Crazy', a Haley original, became the first charting rock'n'roll record in history, going to No. 15. After a 1954 recording of 'Rock Around The Clock' was used to capture the mood of disaffected youth in a new film, *Blackboard Jungle* in 1955, the track stormed to No. 1 – and stayed there for eight weeks.

Haley and his band appeared in films, *Rock Around The Clock* and *Don't Knock The Rock* (both 1956), and had further big hits with 'Rock–A–Beatin' Boogie' (1955), 'See You Later, Alligator' and 'The Saints Rock'n'Roll' (both 1956). The band toured Britain to a (literally) riotous reception in 1957. UK fans sent 'Rock Around The Clock' into the charts on three different occasions: 1954, 1968 and 1974. But, there was a new generation – the Presleys, Cochrans and Berrys – following in Haley's pioneering footsteps and The Comets got left behind. Haley died on 9 February 1981 in Harlingen, Texas.

GENRES
Rock'n'Roll, R&B, Country, Rockabilly

ACTIVE YEARS
1946–80

CLASSIC RECORDINGS
'Crazy Man, Crazy', 'Rock Around The Clock', 'Shake, Rattle And Roll', 'See You Later, Alligator', *Rock Around The Country*

158

JIMI HENDRIX

GUITAR, VOCALS

With his pioneering use of fuzz, feedback and distortion used in tandem with a God-given talent, Jimi Hendrix expanded and redefined the range of the electric guitar and became one of rock's greatest superstars, all within the space of just four years. Born in Seattle, Washington, the left-handed Johnny Allen Hendrix (renamed James Marshall by his father Al Hendrix) taught himself to play guitar. He drew on blues influences such as Robert Johnson, Howlin' Wolf, Muddy Waters, T-Bone Walker and B.B. King, as well as soul legend Curtis Mayfield and early rockers like Buddy Holly. He played in a couple of high-school bands, as well as for another outfit during a US Army stint. In November 1962 he was discharged due to injury, at which point he began working as a session guitarist under the names of both Maurice and Jimmy James.

Assignments followed with the soul/R&B likes of Sam Cooke, King Curtis, Ike & Tina Turner, The Isley Brothers, Little Richard and John Hammond Jr, but Hendrix opted to switch from sideman to lead guitarist in his own band, Jimmy James & The Blue Flames. Playing gigs around New York City's Greenwich Village throughout late 1965 and much of 1966, Hendrix was spotted by Animals' bassist Chas Chandler during a performance at Café Wha? in July 1966. A couple of months later Chandler persuaded Hendrix to relocate to London, which back then represented the centre of the creative/cultural universe.

After quitting The Animals, and in partnership with the group's manager, Mike Jeffery, Chandler signed Hendrix to a management contract and helped create The Jimi Hendrix Experience with guitarist Noel Redding on bass and the highly talented Mitch Mitchell (born John Mitchell) on drums.

A METEORIC RISE TO FAME

In these post-Internet days, it's inconceivable that someone could burst on to the British music scene and not already be a known quantity. But what was so astonishing about Jimi Hendrix was the fact that no one in Britain

knew him from Adam. Twelve months after touchdown, he'd surpassed the ruling triumvirate of Clapton, Beck and Townshend as the world's most flamboyant and influential rock guitarist – bar none.

The Experience's performances were creating a major buzz on the London scene, and they also hit the UK Top 10 three times during the first half of 1967 with the singles 'Hey Joe', 'Purple Haze' and 'The Wind Cries Mary', all produced by Chas Chandler and included on Hendrix's outstanding debut album *Are You Experienced?* (1967). Displaying not only the artist's stunningly virtuosic talents as a guitarist, which melded an assortment of high-volume sonic effects with lightning-fast fingerwork, but also the breadth of his previously unknown abilities as a songwriter, this record ran the gamut from tender ballads to mind-blowing, psychedelic fusions of rock, pop, blues and soul, all wedded to Hendrix's distinctively husky vocals. Combined with his sensational appearance at the Monterey Pop Festival in June 1967, he became a superstar in his home country as well as overseas. It had taken him just nine months.

Onstage the innately shy Hendrix ignited audiences with his breathtaking musicianship and willingness to put on a show, featuring such antics as setting fire to his guitar, while in the studio engineer Eddie Kramer helped realize Jimi's sonic vision by pushing the technological envelope to its absolute limits, as evidenced on *Axis: Bold As Love* (1967) and the double-album *Electric Ladyland* (1968), including self-penned tracks like 'Little Wing', 'Voodoo Chile' and 'Crosstown Traffic', as well as his definitive cover of Bob Dylan's 'All Along The Watchtower'.

A TIME OF UNREST

Opting to return to America halfway through the *Electric Ladyland* sessions, Hendrix parted ways with Chas Chandler, the co-producer having grown tired of his protégé's increasingly time-consuming approach to recording and penchant for populating the studio with assorted friends and hangers-on. Hereafter, the last two years of Jimi's life would be characterized by personal and professional unrest. He folded The Experience in June 1969 and formed the funkier, all-black Band Of Gypsies with old army colleague/musical sidekick Billy Cox on bass and Buddy Miles (born George Miles) on drums.

This was the trio that appeared at Woodstock (Hendrix's erratic performance was salvaged by his unforgettable and then-controversial rendition of 'The Star Spangled Banner') and on the self-titled live album that was culled from performances at New York's Fillmore East on New Year's Eve, 1969, and New Year's Day, 1970. Nevertheless, The Gypsies' standard of musicianship could not match that of Experience members Mitch Mitchell and Noel Redding.

A LEGEND DIES

The Jimi Hendrix Experience was briefly reformed in early 1970. Billy Cox again replaced Redding on bass to tour the world with Hendrix and Mitchell while work was in progress on a fourth album, tentatively titled *First Rays Of The New Rising Sun*. Hendrix's death in London from drugs-related causes on 18 September of that year would prevent its completion, yet the existing tracks and numerous other unreleased recordings would posthumously see the light of day.

Hendrix's sound and style has continued to be both inimitable and influential; Robin Trower, Frank Marino of Mahogany Rush, Uli Jon Roth and others have continued to show his inspiration in their music. *The Radio 1 Sessions* (1989), BBC recordings form his early London years, was a genuine addition to his catalogue, but constant reworkings of his albums, latterly by his family, have not served his legacy well.

GENRES

Hard Rock, Blues Rock, Psychedelic Rock

ACTIVE YEARS

1963–70

CLASSIC RECORDINGS

Are You Experienced?, *Axis: Bold As Love*, *Electric Ladyland*, 'Voodoo Child (Slight Return)', 'The Star Spangled Banner' (Live At Woodstock)

BUDDY HOLLY

GUITAR, SINGER/SONGWRITER

Buddy Holly was born Charles Hardin Holley in Lubbock, Texas. The bespectacled singer–songwriter scored hits both with The Crickets, whose first hit, 'That'll Be The Day', became a US No. 1 in the summer of 1957, and under his own name. This dual success continued with 'Peggy Sue', a Holly track; then a couple of Crickets' releases, 'Oh Boy!' backed with 'Not Fade Away' and 'Maybe Baby'; followed by two Holly numbers, 'Listen To Me' and 'Rave On'. New bassist and guitarist Joe B. Mauldin and Niki Sullivan joined Holly and drummer Jerry Allison. In March 1958, The Crickets toured Britain, and two avid spectators at their Liverpool gig were teenagers John Lennon and Paul McCartney. Several years on their compositions rang with Holly's influence, while McCartney would later buy the publishing rights to his catalogue.

Holly and The Crickets went their separate ways in 1958. In 1959, Buddy headlined the 'Winter Dance Party' tour. After a gig at Clear Lake, Iowa, he chartered a plane, and died with Ritchie Valens and the Big Bopper when it crashed in snowy conditions on 3 February. While Holly's tragic death left so much potential unfulfilled, his legacy would influence rockers and singer/songwriters alike, from Bob Dylan to Elvis Costello, The Rolling Stones to Paul Simon.

GENRES

Rock'n'Roll, Rockabilly

ACTIVE YEARS

1956–59

CLASSIC RECORDINGS

'That'll Be The Day', 'Peggy Sue', 'Oh Boy!', 'Not Fade Away', *The Chirping Crickets*, *Buddy Holly*, 'It Doesn't Matter Anymore', 'True Love Ways'

TOP 100
ROCK ARTISTS

HOWLIN' WOLF

GUITAR, VOCALS

Howlin' Wolf was born Chester Burnett in West Point, Mississippi, and learned the blues from Charley Patton and harmonica from Sonny Boy Williamson, who married his half–sister. After the Army, he began performing around West Memphis, Arkansas, wowing fans with his aggressive vocals and newfangled electric guitar. Promoting himself on local radio, he was heard by Sam Phillips, who cut Wolf's first sides at Phillips' Memphis Recording Service. Phillips played the results to Chess Records.

For Chess, Wolf had hits with 'Evil' and 'Smokestack Lightnin''. Wolf's career headed to a new level in 1960 when he was teamed with writer Willie Dixon. The combination produced a spate of mid–1960s hits, including 'I Ain't Superstitious', 'Back Door Man', 'Spoonful' and 'Wang Dang Doodle'. Wolf toured Europe and became an inspiration to The Rolling Stones, whose version of 'Little Red Rooster' reached No. 1 in Britain in 1964. Indeed, when The Stones were asked in 1965 to appear on the US TV pop show *Shindig!*, they did so on the proviso that Wolf also featured as special guest. Wolf's material was also recorded by The Doors, Cream and Jeff Beck. His later solo albums were not as successful, and in the 1970s his health began to fail. He died in a Veterans' Administration Hospital in 1976.

GENRES

Electric Blues, Chicago Blues

ACTIVE YEARS

1951–76

CLASSIC RECORDINGS

'How Many More Years', 'Evil', 'Smokestack Lightnin'', 'Spoonful', 'Back Door Man', 'Little Red Rooster', 'I Ain't Superstitious'

iRON MAiDEN

VOCAL/iNSTRUMENTAL GROUP

Original lead vocalist Paul Di'Anno led this East London heavy metal outfit to No. 4 on the UK chart in 1980 with their self-titled debut album. New singer Bruce Dickinson went three places better with 1982's *The Number Of The Beast*. The band soon became Britain's top metal group, with their hard rocking, if slightly tongue-in-cheek, approach. Steve Harris (bass, vocals), Dave Murray (guitar), Adrian Smith (guitar) and Nicko McBrain (drums) are the most enduring members of Iron Maiden, though both Dickinson and Smith left and returned. Between 1985 and 1995 the band's singles and albums were rarely out of the Top 10 in the UK, or Top 20 in the US. Particular highlights include the 1988 concept album *Seventh Son Of A Seventh Son* and the bullet-spitting rock of 1990's *No Prayer For The Dying*, which spawned the band's only UK No. 1 single 'Bring Your Daughter To The Slaughter'.

Named after a medieval torture device, Iron Maiden look set to rock on for as long as they desire, with founder and chief songwriter Harris still very motivated. Dickinson, who rejoined the band in 1999 after five years solo, pilots airliners when not touring. He also flies the band to many of their dates in his Boeing 757 Ed Force One, named after mascot Eddie the Head.

GENRES

Heavy Metal

ACTIVE YEARS

1976–present

CLASSIC RECORDINGS

The Number Of The Beast, Piece Of Mind, Powerslave, Seventh Son Of A Seventh Son, No Prayer For The Dying

MICHAEL JACKSON

VOCALS

The youngest member of The Jackson Five, Michael Jackson signed a solo deal in 1971 with Motown Records, aged just 13. Within a year he had overtaken the Jackson Five on the strength of two US Top 5 singles – 'Got To Be There' and 'Rockin' Robin' – followed by a No. 1 with 'Ben'. After that his career stalled because of the sub-standard material he was given. In 1975, he switched to Epic but his career continued to stagnate until 1977 when he teamed up with producer Quincy Jones. Their first album together, *Off The Wall* (1979), reached No. 3 in the US charts and Jackson became the first solo artist to have four US Top 10 singles from one album. More significantly, *Off The Wall* stayed in the US charts for a year (more than three years in the UK).

THRILLING SUCCESS

Jackson's next album, *Thriller* (1982), eclipsed the high standards of *Off The Wall* with seven US Top 10 singles including two No. 1s – 'Billie Jean' and 'Beat It' – and three more that went Top 5. Jackson also won an unprecedented eight Grammy Awards in 1983. The album, which stayed at No. 1 in America for 37 weeks and was still in the charts 21 months later, again straddled different genres with consummate skill. The album was also visually choreographed by videos, including a mini-epic for 'Thriller'. As a result Jackson became the first black artist to get regular exposure on MTV and his dancing and fashion quirks became as iconic as his music. *Thriller* was an impossible album to follow and while *Bad* (1987) could not compete in chart terms, it still sold 22 million copies and produced a record five US No. 1 singles.

Dangerous (1991), co-produced by Teddy Riley, topped the US charts for four weeks and 'Black Or White' was No. 1 for seven weeks. The *Dangerous* world tour was his biggest yet but it ended prematurely in 1993 when Jackson was engulfed in scandal. Fans had always been tolerant of his eccentricities but allegations of child abuse caused lasting damage to his reputation.

TOP 100
ROCK ARTISTS

HIStory (1995) was a double CD of greatest hits and new songs, which was backed by a massive marketing campaign and was another US and UK No. 1, along with the single 'You Are Not Alone'. But Jackson was now more popular in the rest of the world than the US; a fact that became obvious when his *HIStory* world tour included no American shows apart from Hawaii.

A TROUBLED STAR

Blood On The Dancefloor (1997) featured remixes from *HIStory* and new songs. The title track was a UK No. 1, although it failed to make the US Top 40. *Invincible* (2001) was Jackson's first album of all-new material since *Dangerous* and debuted at No. 1 in the US, selling over 11 million copies worldwide. But controversy was never far away. He inexplicably dangled his child over a hotel balcony in Berlin; an image-restoring TV documentary, *Living With Michael Jackson*, had the opposite effect; and in 2005 he faced more child abuse allegations, this time in court. He was acquitted, but his mysterious death in June 2009 on the eve of a much-trumpeted live comeback saw him deified by millions of devastated followers.

GENRES

Pop, Dance, Rock, R&B, Soul, New Jack Swing

ACTIVE YEARS

1964–2009

CLASSIC RECORDINGS

'Don't Stop 'Til You Get Enough', *Thriller*, 'Billy Jean', 'Bad', 'Black Or White'

JETHRO TULL
VOCAL/INSTRUMENTAL GROUP

While this group – originally Ian Anderson (vocals, flute), Mick Abrahams (guitar), Glenn Cornick (bass) and Clive Bunker (drums) – rose on the crest of the British 'blues boom' in the late 1960s, they absorbed many other musical idioms, principally via composer Anderson. (The Tull of the band's title was a pioneering English agriculturalist, though many assumed it was Anderson.) The image of Anderson's matted hair, vagrant attire and antics with his flute during early TV appearances was not easily forgotten, for, as well as being a popular album act (especially after the second one, *Stand Up* (1969), sold well in North America), they were also mainstream pop stars by 1969. Released that year, 'Living In The Past' all but topped the UK chart and reached No. 11 in the US chart. Such entries, however, dried up by 1971 when *Aqualung*, a 'concept' album, appeared.

By the 1980s, the group had become Anderson and Martin Barre (guitar) plus backing musicians whose living depended mostly upon US consumers' continued liking for 1987's Grammy-winning *Crest Of A Knave* and whatever other albums the financially secure Anderson chose to record. A fortieth-anniversary tour in 2008 brought out many former members to play some of the old songs in guest appearances. Live shows are similar to watching a panto, but enthusiastically attended and applauded by a faithful worldwide following, which now includes India.

GENRES

Progressive Rock, Folk Rock, Hard Rock

ACTIVE YEARS

1967–present

CLASSIC RECORDINGS

Stand Up, 'Living In The Past', *Aqualung, Thick As A Brick, A Passion Play, Crest Of A Knave*

ELTON JOHN

PIANO, VOCALS

Elton John was one of the most extrovert performers of the 1970s and has sold over 250 million records worldwide. Born Reginald Kenneth Dwight, he won a part-time piano scholarship to London's Royal Academy Of Music at the age of 11. In 1966 the band Bluesology became a back-up band for Long John Baldry and Dwight changed his name, taking the Christian names of John Baldry and saxophone player Elton Dean. He left in 1967 and teamed with lyricist Bernie Taupin. Elton's first album, *Empty Sky* (1969) showed potential, but it was *Elton John* (1970) that lit the fuse, particularly in America after rave reviews for his debut at the Los Angeles Troubadour. A Top 10 single with 'Your Song' helped the album go Top 5.

A PROLIFIC PERFORMER

Between 1971 and 1976 Elton released over a dozen albums, seven of which went to No. 1 in the US along with five No. 1 singles. While the UK chart statistics were not as impressive (four No. 1 albums, one No. 1 single), he scored just as many hits. There were four Elton albums in 1971: *Tumbleweed Connection* (which reflected Taupin's fascination with the American West), the live *17-11-70*, the film soundtrack *Friends* and the lush and haunting *Madman Across The Water*.

The hits started to flow in 1972, launched by 'Rocket Man' and 'Honky Cat' from *Honky Chateau*, followed by 'Crocodile Rock' and 'Daniel' from *Don't Shoot Me I'm Only The Piano Player* (1973), 'Goodbye Yellow Brick Road', 'Candle In The Wind' and 'Bennie And The Jets' from *Goodbye Yellow Brick Road* (1973) and 'Don't Let The Sun Go Down On Me' and 'The Bitch Is Back' from *Caribou* (1974).

Elton's flamboyant shows – his outrageous glasses got bigger in proportion to the venue – made him one of the top live attractions. Elton premiered *Captain Fantastic And The Brown Dirt Cowboy* (1975) at London's Wembley Stadium.

After his first UK No. 1 single 'Don't Go Breaking My Heart' (a duet with Kiki Dee) and the double album *Blue Moves* (1976), Elton took a break and bought Watford Football Club.

A NEW CHAPTER

A Single Man (1978) marked a complete career change. He disbanded his partnership with Taupin (they would work together again later), had an instrumental hit with 'Song For Guy' and generally broadened his perspectives, becoming the first pop star to tour Russia and reorganizing his career around his life rather than vice versa. The hits continued, but he was becoming as famous for his lifestyle as his music. Elton faced up to his homosexuality, as well as his various addictions, but his popularity never waned. He continued to write major film themes ('Can You Feel The Love Tonight' from *The Lion King* in 1994) and collaborate with other singers. All proceeds from his singles go to his AIDS foundation, which also benefits from the annual 'Elton's Closet' auction.

Proof of Elton's place in the nation's affections came when he sang 'Candle In The Wind' with revised lyrics at the funeral of Princess Diana in Westminster Abbey in 1997. It became the world's biggest-selling single with sales of over 33 million. In 1998 he was knighted by the Queen. In 2004, Elton started a three-year Las Vegas residency, alternating with Celine Dion, and in 2005 he appeared at Live 8, 20 years after he had appeared at Band Aid.

GENRES

Pop, Soft Rock, Glam Rock

ACTIVE YEARS

1963–present

CLASSIC RECORDINGS

'Rocket Man', 'Daniel', *Goodbye Yellow Brick Road*, 'Candle In The Wind', *Caribou*, 'Don't Go Breaking My Heart', 'I'm Still Standing', 'Nikita'

JANIS JOPLIN

VOCALS

During a troubled adolescence in Texas, Joplin sang in regional clubs before moving to California. Here she emerged as the focal point of San Francisco's Big Brother & The Holding Company, sounding weary, cynical and knowing beyond her years. They were a hit of 1967's Monterey Pop Festival where they stole the show alongside fellow San Francisco bands like Jefferson Airplane. Her raspy vocals betrayed a hard-living lifestyle, but Jack Daniel's gave way to hard drugs and this, mixed with low self-esteem, would be her undoing.

In 1968, Janis began a solo career that was both triumphant and tragic. Three big concerts in London, Newport and New Orleans launched her solo debut *I Got Dem Ol' Kozmic Blues Again, Mama!* (1969), after which she formed her own Full Tilt Boogie Band. She then topped both the US album and singles chart with, respectively, *Pearl* and 'Me And Bobby McGee' (both 1971). Success was bittersweet as it came shortly after her drug-induced death in October 1970. She has inspired generations since, the likes of Bonnie Tyler namechecking her as an influence. Indeed, she could well have been the greatest female singer of all time.

GENRES

Blues Rock, Hard Rock, Psychedelic Rock

ACTIVE YEARS

1963–70

CLASSIC RECORDINGS

Cheap Thrills, 'Ball And Chain', *I Got Dem Ol' Kozmic Blues Again, Mama!*, *Pearl*, 'Me And Bobby McGee', 'Mercedes Benz', 'Get It While You Can'

B.B. KING

GUITAR, VOCALS

Riley B. King, from Indianola, Mississippi, is arguably the last surviving authentic blues artist. In 2009, *Time* magazine named him No. 3 on its list of the 10 best electric guitarists of all time. An orphan, he took up guitar aged 15, busking on street corners and turning professional after US military service. In 1947, he hitched to Memphis in the hope of getting on Sonny Boy Williamson's show. There, he worked on a local radio station, acquiring his B.B. ('Blues Boy') epithet and also working with Bobby Bland and Johnny Ace. He lived with cousin Bukka White, one of his early influences along with T-Bone Walker, Charlie Christian's single-string runs and Lester Young's evocative saxophone.

THE DEFINING DECADE

First recording in 1949, King's breakthrough came with 1951's US R&B chart-topper 'Three O'Clock Blues'. It was this decade that saw him produce his most influential music, notably songs like 'Did You Ever Love A Woman', 'You Upset Me Baby', Robert Nighthawk's 'Sweet Little Angel' and 'Every Day I Have The Blues'.

An inability to sing and play at the same time saw him adopt a call and response routine with his guitar, the to-ing and fro-ing effect echoing both gospel preaching and the chants from the cotton fields. Another 'limitation', a lack of facility at slide playing, also led to him developing a musical trademark – this time a unique mix of vibrato and sustain, which, combined with almost constantly bending notes on a single string, resulted in a guitar sound that was very much his own. He's never used a vibrato tailpiece.

R&B hits continued, but after signing with ABC-Paramount circa 1964, he regularly crossed over to the US pop singles chart with the likes of 'The Thrill Is Gone', also making the US pop album chart from 1968, with big albums like *Live And Well* and *Completely Well* (both 1969), *Live In Cook County Jail* (1971) and 1974's gold-certified

Together For The First Time ... Live with Bobby Bland. He experimented with soul and even country, adding a jazz edge to collaborations with The Crusaders. His albums were still being nominated for Grammies half a century after his recording debut. His appeal became universal.

A GRUELLING SCHEDULE

King toured relentlessly, and was said to have played 300 shows per year between the mid–1950s and the late 1970s. (He flew himself to gigs until the age of 70, being a licensed pilot.) He has also battled diabetes, which hospitalized him briefly in 1990, and is a spokesperson to raise awareness for the condition. King still performs and records, and has frequently guested with younger blues guitarists such as Eric Clapton, even sharing a 1989 hit single, 'When Love Comes To Town', with U2 – his first UK Top 10 entry in a long career. A career–defining *King Of The Blues* box set was issued in 1992, while the following year saw him share the spotlight with Robert Cray, Etta James, Buddy Guy and more in *Blues Summit* (1993).

At an age when most legends were hanging up their instruments, B.B. King played on with his guitar, Lucille. The Boy from Beale Street opened a blues club on that very thoroughfare in the early 1990s and, while he was no longer busking for nickels and dimes, he believed business would continue to be good. 'As long as people have problems,' he explained, 'the blues can never die.'

GENRES

Memphis Blues, R&B, Soul Blues

ACTIVE YEARS

1947–present

CLASSIC RECORDINGS

'Three O'Clock Blues', 'Please Love Me', 'You Upset Me Baby', 'Sweet Little Angel', 'Sweet Sixteen', 'The Thrill Is Gone', 'When Love Comes To Town'

THE KINKS

VOCAL/INSTRUMENTAL GROUP

One of the more popular bands of the 'British Invasion' and a considerable influence on 1990s groups such as Blur and Oasis, The Kinks went through numerous line-up changes but were always led by singer/songwriter Ray Davies, with guitarist brother Dave alongside. Following a couple of unsuccessful releases, The Kinks' 'You Really Got Me' hit the top of the UK charts in 1964 and made the US Top 10. Featuring Ray's idiosyncratic vocal style, the record was distinguished by Dave's fierce, distorted, proto-punk power chords.

As the 1960s progressed, Ray Davies' compositions would become more introspective and whimsically English, as characterized by such classic UK hits as 'Dedicated Follower Of Fashion', 'Sunny Afternoon', 'Dead End Street', 'Waterloo Sunset', 'Autumn Almanac' and 'Days'. Critically acclaimed albums included *The Village Green Preservation Society* (1968), a nostalgic reflection on Ray's favoured English traditions, and 1969 concept album *Arthur (Or The Decline And Fall Of The British Empire)*. Unfortunately, sales were modest. The Kinks enjoyed renewed success in America with albums *Sleepwalker* (1977), *Misfits* (1978), *Low Budget* (1979) and the aptly titled *Give The People What They Want* (1981), touring arenas to sell-out crowds. The group was inducted into the Rock And Roll Hall Of Fame in 1990.

GENRES

Rock, Pop

ACTIVE YEARS

1964–96

CLASSIC RECORDINGS

'You Really Got Me', 'All Day And All Of The Night', 'Tired Of Waiting For You', 'Dedicated Follower Of Fashion', 'Sunny Afternoon', 'Lola', 'Apeman'

LED ZEPPELIN

VOCAL/INSTRUMENTAL GROUP

The biggest heavy metal band of the 1970s, Led Zeppelin left an indelible mark that is still felt a quarter of a century later. The band was put together in London in 1968 by guitarist Jimmy Page (born James Patrick Page), singer Robert Plant, bassist John Paul Jones (born John Baldwin) and drummer John Bonham (born John Henry Bonham).

Page was an in-demand session player in the mid-1960s and joined The Yardbirds in 1966, playing alongside Jeff Beck. By early 1968 the band was in decline and Page began planning with road manager Peter Grant to build on the success Cream had achieved with their heavy blues-rock. When The Yardbirds broke up in 1968 he recruited Jones, another prominent session musician. They contacted singer Terry Riley who was unavailable but recommended Plant, a member of the Midlands group Band Of Joy. He in turn recommended drummer Bonham, and Led Zeppelin were born.

UNPRECEDENTED ARTISTIC CONTROL

They recorded their debut album at London's Olympic Studios in just 30 hours and Grant took the tapes to America. He negotiated a contract with Atlantic Records that gave the band a £200,000 advance and complete artistic control – unprecedented for an unknown group. *Led Zeppelin* (1969) contained heavy, stylized versions of Willie Dixon's 'You Shook Me' and 'I Can't Quit You Baby' and self-written tracks like the frenetic 'Communication Breakdown' and the slow-building, explosive 'Dazed And Confused' that featured Page playing guitar with a violin bow.

Led Zeppelin gradually climbed the US and UK album charts, eventually reaching the Top 10 without help from singles or TV appearances. As a result, the group remained 'exclusive' to the burgeoning rock audience. When *Led Zeppelin II* was released in November 1969 it quickly rose to No. 1 in the US and UK. *Led Zeppelin II* was recorded at various

studios in breaks between tours but was mixed in a single weekend. The opening 'Whole Lotta Love' was Led Zeppelin's manifesto condensed into five and a half minutes – a dynamic riff, vocal preening and a pared-down chorus with guitar echo effects, followed by a crazed middle section. In addition to ferocious rockers like 'Heartbreaker' there were expansive acoustic songs like 'Ramble On'.

Led Zeppelin maintained a punishing schedule through 1970, then took a break to prepare material for their next album at an isolated Welsh cottage called Bron-y-Aur. *Led Zeppelin III* was released in October 1970 with advance orders that sent it to the top of the US and UK charts. It contained the fierce 'Immigrant Song' and the heavyweight blues 'Since I've Been Loving You', but sales failed to match *Led Zeppelin II*.

AN EPIC ALBUM IS BORN

At the end of the year the band were back in the studio working on their next album. *Led Zeppelin IV* came out in October 1971 and is widely regarded as their finest album. They successfully blended the various elements of their character – the powerful 'Black Dog' and 'Rock And Roll', the gentler 'Going To California' and the stark 'When The Levee Breaks' – and brought them all together on the epic 'Stairway To Heaven'. Ironically, the album failed to top the US charts, stalling at No. 2, but sales outstripped earlier releases. Zeppelin played sell-out tours of Australia, Japan, Britain and Europe, breaking US box-office records set by The Beatles.

Houses Of The Holy (1973) left critics lukewarm, but was a No. 1 album around the world. By now Led Zeppelin were touring America in a private jet with their logo on the side, and tales of their excesses were entering folklore. At the beginning of 1974 they formed their own record label, Swansong, and spent much of the year working on the album. They returned with the double album *Physical Graffiti* (1975), which received universal acclaim and prompted another massive American tour. But in August 1975 Plant was involved in a car accident and suffered multiple fractures. Touring plans were cancelled and the band worked instead on their next album, *Presence*, released in April 1976. That was followed by a film and live album, *The Song Remains The Same* (1976).

Led Zeppelin started their first American tour for nearly two years in April 1977 with their popularity undiminished. When the band arrived in New Orleans on 26 July, Plant was told that his five-year-old son had died and group operations were suspended until late 1978 when they reconvened at ABBA's Stockholm studios. *In Through The Out Door* (1979) topped the US charts for seven weeks.

AND THEN THERE WERE THREE

The band were rehearsing for an American tour when John Bonham was found dead on 25 September 1980 after drinking more than a bottle of vodka. In December the remaining band members announced that they 'could not continue as we were'. An album of unreleased recordings, *Coda*, was issued in 1982. Jones retired from live performance, undertaking various low-key projects. Plant pursued a solo career releasing eight albums and revisiting his R&B roots with side project The Honeydrippers. Page recorded solo albums and linked up with Paul Rodgers, David Coverdale and The Black Crowes for projects.

In 1985 the three surviving members performed as Led Zeppelin at Live Aid with drummers Phil Collins and Tony Thompson and again in 1993 at Atlantic Records' fortieth-anniversary concert to commemorate founder Ahmet Ertegun's passing. In 1994 Page and Plant teamed up for an MTV show, *Unledded*, featuring reworked Zeppelin songs with Middle Eastern and North African musical influences. The Zeppelin legacy has been periodically boosted by live recordings and DVDs, while a one-off live reunion at London's O2 in 2007 with Bonham's son Jason was massively oversubscribed.

GENRES

Hard Rock, Heavy Metal, Blues Rock, Folk Rock

ACTIVE YEARS

1968–80

CLASSIC RECORDINGS

Led Zeppelin II, 'Whole Lotta Love', *Led Zeppelin IV*, 'Black Dog', 'Stairway To Heaven', *Houses Of The Holy*, *Physical Graffiti*, *Presence*

JERRY LEE LEWIS

PIANO, VOCALS

Jerry Lee Lewis briefly shared a studio with Elvis Presley in the late 1950s. The music he consigned to tape while in the Sun Studios was released to a waiting world who had never heard anything quite like it. Writer Nick Tosches, who was Lewis's biographer in 1982's *Hellfire*, compared the two: 'Presley was the guileless star-god who rendered rock'n'roll acceptable to the masses. Then there came Jerry Lee, the dark angel who personified all that was hellish and fearsome in rock'n'roll.'

Lewis was brought up in Ferriday, Louisiana. He played piano at the local Assembly of God church, instilling a guilt he would never free himself from. He had trained to be a Pentecostal preacher alongside cousin Jimmy Swaggart, who thought the devil had taken control of him. Jerry Lee was indeed a wild youth and had married bigamously for the second time at the age of 17.

AN INSTANT HIT

After signing to Sun in 1957, Lewis, noted for his percussive piano style, opened his account with two million-selling US Top 3 hits, 'Whole Lot Of Shakin' Going On' and 'Great Balls Of Fire'. It was when the latter reached No. 1 in 1958 that Britain sat up and took notice; 'Breathless' was a Top 10 follow-up and, by the time movie theme 'High School Confidential' had made it four in a row, Lewis's fame was assured.

Major media controversy was to follow, however. During a 1958 UK tour it was discovered that his wife, who was also his cousin, was only 13 years old (legal in parts of the US, unacceptable in the UK). This blighted his pop career, and back home there would be no further hits until 'What'd I Say' reached No. 30 and heralded a short-lived 1961 comeback. But country music offered him a safe haven and, from the late 1960s onwards, he combined the rockabilly that made him

famous with country, becoming a major US star with over 60 US country hits, many making the Top 10, including his chart-topping 1972 revival of 'Chantilly Lace'.

The manic piano-player has since survived numerous personal tragedies, including the death of two sons a decade apart, the deaths of two wives in strange circumstances, and serious illnesses that have affected him personally. Some problems were self-inflicted. In 1976 he shot his bass player Butch Owens, thankfully not fatally, and weeks later was arrested for drunk driving after putting his Rolls-Royce in a ditch. Just 10 hours after his release he was arrested again, this time outside Graceland where he was wielding a loaded pistol and demanding to see Elvis.

A COUNTRY STAR

Despite these problems, his country hits continued with 'Let's Put It Back Together Again' and 'Middle Age Crazy', both aptly titled. In 1981 he sued his record label Elektra after they attempted to break his contract. He was in a Memphis hospital at the time having had extensive stomach surgery. The mid-1990s saw him signed to punk label Sire and attempting yet another comeback. The standout track of *Young Blood* (1995) was 'I'll Never Get Out Of This World Alive' by Hank Williams, one of the few artists he considered his equal.

Jerry Lee's epic, event-filled career inspired a 1989 biopic, inevitably titled *Great Balls Of Fire*, in which Dennis Quaid played him. The King may be dead, but The Killer and his music live on.

GENRES

Rock'n'Roll, Country

ACTIVE YEARS

1954–present

CLASSIC RECORDINGS

'Whole Lot Of Shakin' Going On', 'Great Balls Of Fire', 'High School Confidential', 'Sweet Little Sixteen', 'Good Golly Miss Molly', 'Chantilly Lace'

LITTLE RICHARD

PIANO, VOCALS

When you're one of 12 children, you either seek attention or slope off into a corner and sulk. Richard Wayne Penniman, otherwise known as Little Richard, was and has always been an unashamed attention-seeker. Raised in a religious Georgian family where his grandfather and two uncles were preachers, he started recording for RCA in 1951 after winning a talent contest. Chart success followed his signing with Specialty Records, where influential bandleader Bumps Blackwell produced a series of classic rock'n'roll tracks between 1955 and 1958. Previous recorded efforts had failed to capture Richard's on-stage excitement, so Blackwell decided to record him live in the studio with session musicians sympathetic to his music. Many of these were the same New Orleans crew behind Fats Domino and Lloyd Price.

A ROCK LEADER

The first release was 1955's 'Tutti Frutti', a million-seller and the last of nine songs recorded in a six-hour session. It gave the rock world its first catchphrase – 'Awopbopaloobop alopbamboom!' – and was something of a lewd nursery rhyme in lyrical terms. Cooked up between takes, it was an unlikely but primally exciting sound that reached No. 17 in the US chart. The next three years brought further sales successes in 1956's million-selling 'Long Tall Sally' and 'Rip It Up', 1957's 'Lucille' and 'Keep A Knockin'' and 1958's 'Good Golly Miss Molly', among others. These are songs that, over the years have been revived by acts as diverse as The Beatles, The Everly Brothers and Bruce Springsteen.

The self-styled 'Georgia Peach' created the blueprint for star-struck piano-players everywhere, including one Reginald Dwight who caught him live at Harrow's Granada Cinema on a UK package tour. The future Elton John wasn't the only one to be impressed, as appearances in several rock exploitation movies won the hyperactive, hollering piano-man a worldwide audience.

He cut a distinctive figure with his baggy suits, pencil–thin moustache, mascara and six–inch pompadour. He played the piano standing up and his supercharged performances stole the show in films like *Don't Knock The Rock* (1957), *The Girl Can't Help It* (1956) and *Mister Rock'n'Roll* (1957). There was an element of standard showbiz about him – after a wild explosion of rock'n'roll, he bowed to the audience as though he had been playing a Chopin minuet.

Otis Redding and James Brown were among contemporary black performers to borrow elements of Little Richard's style, while Paul McCartney, who backed him with the early Beatles at a Hamburg engagement, became adept at duplicating Richard's falsetto on stage at the Star Club. The Beatles eventually recorded 'Long Tall Sally' in 1974. Meanwhile, a young Bob Dylan told his school yearbook in Hibbing, Minnesota, that his ambition in life was 'to join Little Richard'.

ROCK AND RELIGION

While touring Australia in 1957, Little Richard abandoned the music business. He dedicated his life to God, either because he saw seeing the Russian Sputnik space rocket as a divine sign to change his behaviour, or because he survived a bumpy plane trip and swore if he got out alive he would change. He studied to become a preacher, recording only gospel music. He returned to the fray in the mid–1960s with a young, unknown Jimi Hendrix as part of his US road band. Rumour has it Jimi was sacked by Little Richard for grabbing attention with his colourful shirts. Sax star Junior Walker and keyboardist Billy Preston were among others stars to pass through the ranks.

The divide between rock and religion that had led Richard to throw his rings off the Sydney Harbour Bridge would continue to dog the God–fearing piano–thumper as he retired and returned frequently. One such return to rock'n'roll was on the Vee Jay label – the label that launched The Beatles' American career – in 1964–65 when he remade all his classic hits of the 1950s. He had been booked to tour the UK with Sam Cooke as a gospel singer, but, having seen Cooke get a standing ovation, he reverted to rock'n'roll to upstage him. His last hit came in 1964 in the shape of 'Bama Lama Bama Loo', a fairly obvious attempt to recreate the primal excitement of 'Tutti Frutti' that was rendered somewhat passé by the new wave of white pop and rock acts.

While he remained a dynamic live performer and an undoubted legend, Richard's later records rarely matched his 1950s rock'n'roll hits, which sold in huge numbers. An estimated 18 million of his singles were bought during the last half of that decade. The Stones frontman Mick Jagger was a fan and picked up on Richard's effeminate side, which Richard renounced in 1980, declaring 'I used to be a raving homosexual until God changed me.' That said, he had an ex-wife and child in the background so the jury was out on his true leanings.

INSPIRING A GENERATION

The mid-1980s found Little Richard rocking out yet again in the film *Down And Out In Beverly Hills* (1986). He was intent on proving his official biographer, Chas 'Dr Rock' White right when he wrote that Richard 'makes Pavarotti sound like a squeaking mouse'. He was inducted into the Rock And Roll Hall Of Fame in 1986 and won a Lifetime Achievement Grammy seven years later.

Unlike Elvis Presley, who became a mega-successful film star, and Jerry Lee Lewis, who moved sideways into country, Little Richard did not manage his career successfully. He produced his best work during a couple of years in the mid-1950s. Yet he was undoubtedly an innovator who influenced a generation, even if he was unable to build on the foundations his recordings and stage act had laid.

GENRES

Rock'n'Roll, R&B, Soul, Gospel

ACTIVE YEARS

1951–present

CLASSIC RECORDINGS

'Tutti-Frutti', 'Long Tall Sally', 'Rip It Up', 'Lucille', 'Keep A-Knockin'', 'Good Golly, Miss Molly', 'Baby Face'

LYNYRD SKYNYRD

VOCAL/INSTRUMENTAL GROUP

This archetypal Southern rock band came together in Jacksonville, Florida, around the core of Ronnie Van Zant (vocals), Allen Collins (guitar) and Gary Rossington (guitar), plus Billy Powell (keyboards), Larry Junstrom (bass) and Bob Burns (drums). Producer and record label boss Al Kooper discovered them, and tracks like 'Sweet Home Alabama' and the anthemic 'Freebird' placed them firmly into Southern rock history. Supporting The Who on their Quadrophenia Tour broke the band on a national scale, while third release *Nuthin' Fancy* became their first US Top 10 album. Off stage their hellraising lifestyle made them the scourge of hotel security worldwide, while an unique three–axe attack was completed by additional guitarist Steve Gaines alongside Collins and Rossington. Ex–Strawberry Alarm Clock man Ed King also featured.

An air crash shortly before the release of their sixth album *Street Survivors* in 1977 claimed the lives of Van Zant and Gaines. The band continued after a decade's hiatus with Ronnie's younger brother Johnny now toting the microphone. The band's influence on New Country was recognized by *Skynyrd Frynds*, a star–studded tribute album of their songs released in 1994 by top performers from Travis Tritt and Steve Earle to Wynonna Judd.

GENRES

Southern Rock, Hard Rock, Blues Rock

ACTIVE YEARS

1964–77, 1987–present

CLASSIC RECORDINGS

Lynyrd Skynyrd, 'Freebird', *Second Helping*, 'Sweet Home Alabama', *Nuthin' Fancy*, *Gimme Back My Bullets*, *Street Survivors*

MADONNA

VOCALS

The most successful female recording artist of all time, Madonna also reigns supreme as a top female producer and songwriter. Madonna Louise Ciccone spent her formative years in Detroit. After graduating from high school in 1976, she won a dance scholarship to the University of Michigan but dropped out. She sang in two rock groups before recording the demos that brought her to the attention of Sire Records.

First album *Madonna* (1983) was a collection of disco/pop songs remixed by John 'Jellybean' Benitez because Madonna was unhappy with the initial outcome. The album was not a major success on original release, although it received good reviews and 'Holiday' was a British Top 20 hit. But it was *Like A Virgin* (1984) that established Madonna as an international star, its title track becoming her first worldwide smash. Her material was given a commercial sheen by producer Nile Rodgers (of Chic fame) and the album featured another massive hit in 'Material Girl'. Madonna's first UK No. 1 single 'Into The Groove' (from the movie *Desperately Seeking Susan*) was added to the re-release in 1985, the year when she truly became a phenomenon.

THE QUEEN OF POP

On *True Blue* (1986), the newly crowned 'Queen of Pop' took full control of her music, writing or co-writing all the songs and acting as co-producer. The album, featuring 'Papa Don't Preach', 'Open Your Heart' and 'La Isla Bonita', displayed a new maturity and was another blockbuster. Next, Madonna starred in the 1987 film *Who's That Girl* and the soundtrack album featured four of her songs. Her next album proper, *Like A Prayer* (1989), was an adventurous project, incorporating elements of rock, dance, pop, soul and funk. The video for the title track invited controversy over its use of religious imagery, providing Madonna with priceless publicity.

Another busy year, 1990 saw Madonna appear in the movie *Dick Tracy* and release *I'm Breathless*, an album containing the singles 'Vogue' and 'Hanky Panky'. *The Immaculate Collection* (1990), her first greatest hits package, featured two new songs, 'Justify My Love' and 'Rescue Me', whilst other tracks were remixed and edited.

Erotica (1992), an album themed around sexuality, was largely overshadowed by the furore over *Sex*, a controversial coffee-table book. She reacted with a more mainstream work, *Bedtime Stories* (1994), before playing the title role in the film of the Andrew Lloyd Webber/Tim Rice musical *Evita* released in 1996. Madonna then worked with British musician/producer William Orbit on the ambitious *Ray Of Light* (1998), which restored her commercial pre-eminence. The album expertly blended pop with electronica, ambient trance and quasi-psychedelia, whilst the lyrics were largely personal, with Madonna reflecting on her recent motherhood. Further collaborations with Orbit followed on *Music* (2000).

A STYLE ICON

American Life (2003) was a blend of acoustic and techno, but *Confessions On A Dance Floor* (2005) saw a return to straight forward dance music. Meanwhile, her personal life, including marriage to and divorce from film director Guy Ritchie, a dalliance with the Kabbalah religious sect and the adoption of two African children, has latterly attracted more attention than her music. That aside, Madonna's musical influence over the last quarter-century has been incalculable, and may be discerned in almost every female singer from Kylie Minogue to Kelly Clarkson. Her clothes sense has been almost as noticeable, the ripped tights, underwear as outerwear and famous 'conical bra' having been the most noticeable music-based fashion statements since punk.

GENRES

Pop, Dance, Electronic

ACTIVE YEARS

1979–present

CLASSIC RECORDINGS

'Holiday', *Like A Virgin*, 'Like A Virgin', 'Into The Groove', *True Blue*, *Like A Prayer*, *Ray Of Light*, 'Frozen', *Music*

BOB MARLEY

GUITAR, VOCALS

Like Elvis Presley, Bob Marley's name is virtually synonymous with the style of music he pioneered. Despite the passage of time since his death, the reggae superstar still reigns supreme, acknowledged as having almost single-handedly introduced Jamaican music to the world. The European and American markets were conquered as he transformed reggae from the stuff of one-hit wonders to an influential style that was quickly assimilated into the mainstream.

Marley's recording career began in 1962 when he cut his first record, 'Judge Not', for producer Leslie Kong when just 16 years of age. Linking up first with Bunny Livingston, he then encountered Peter 'Tosh' McIntosh and Junior Braithwaite at a singing session organized by neighbour Joe Higgs. The quartet later slimmed to a trio, operating out of Kingston, Jamaica and enjoying great success locally. Producer Clement 'Coxsone' Dodd gave the group their first Jamaican chart-topper with 'Simmer Down'.

DEVELOPING AND MATURING MUSICALLY

In February 1966 Marley followed his mother to the United States, working in a Delaware car factory for six months to amass funds to form his own label, Tuff Gong. He missed Haile Selassie's state visit to his home island, but joined the fast-growing Rastafarian cult inspired by the Ethiopian Emperor. In 1969, Marley worked with producer Lee 'Scratch' Perry who introduced him to the Barrett brothers – Aston (a.k.a. Family Man, on bass) and Carlton (drums) – who would become a vital component of the new Wailers.

Early songs like 'Soul Almighty' bore the unmistakable American soul influence of James Brown and Sam & Dave, but as The Wailers moved on from vocal group to fully fledged band so Marley's writing grew in maturity. Many of his early

TOP 100
ROCK ARTISTS

songs like 'Kaya', 'Four Hundred Years' and 'Keep On Moving' would be revisited on future albums, and some believe it was when in the company of Livingston and Tosh that Marley made his most potent, undiluted music.

Marley travelled to Europe with Johnny Nash, for whom he wrote the hit 'Stir It Up', and made contact with Island Records whose owner Chris Blackwell (himself a white Jamaican) had made a fortune marketing reggae to a European audience. Island provided the funds for The Wailers to return to Jamaica and cut *Catch A Fire* (1973). Marley's music, as supplied on eight-track recording tape, was subtly enhanced to make it more palatable to rock fans. White American session guitarist Wayne Perkins, for instance, was brought in to add to 'Catch A Fire', as was Free's keyboard player Rabbit Bundrick, both at the suggestion of Blackwell.

TAKING CENTRE STAGE

Eric Clapton's 1974 cover version of 'I Shot The Sheriff' raised Marley's profile when it topped the US charts, and 'No Woman No Cry', from *Live At The Lyceum* (1975), proved his chart breakthrough in Britain. By this time Marley held centre stage – and not only in the world of reggae. Livingston and Tosh had quit for solo careers, leaving Bob the undisputed focus of attention like a Jagger or a Springsteen.

The exultant *Exodus* gave Marley his first UK Top 10 chart album in 1977 and, with bands like The Clash and The Police underlining the new-wave's wish to borrow reggae's rebel stance, he was now guaranteed chart records and sell-out concerts wherever he went. This state of affairs would continue until 1979 when, during a tour of the States, he was seen to be ailing. He had been diagnosed with cancer in a toe in 1977 (described at the time as a football injury) and, though he refused to have the toe and part of his right foot amputated, had appeared to be making a recovery. Sadly that was not to be and *Uprising* (1980) was to be his last studio album.

In his last years Bob Marley had spent time in Africa, celebrating Zimbabwe's independence and recording the Afro-centred 'Survival'. Though darker than previous efforts, it made such an impact that even now Wailers music enjoys unprecedented status in the African continent, confirming Marley as the Third World's own – and possibly only – musical superstar.

Since his death in 1981, Marley's reputation and influence has risen steadily, aided by 1984's mega-selling *Legend* collection of his finest Island-label recordings. *Legend* holds the distinction of being the second longest-charting album in the history of the *Billboard* US chart, while worldwide sales exceed 25 million.

LEGACY OF PEACE AND LOVE

In amongst Marley's militant calls to arms and hymns to the Rastafarian religion were more universal calls for peace and love: 'Redemption Song' is one of his most-covered songs, with its evocative plea to 'Emancipate yourselves from mental slavery'. This combination proved the secret of his songwriting success. A major skill was to coat songs with incendiary lyrics like 'Babylon System', 'Get Up Stand Up', 'War' and 'Rat Race' with irresistible grooves; the sweet melodies make the angry lyrics easier to swallow.

Even today, Bob Marley songs appear in the charts with regularity: The Fugees' 1996 cover of 'No Woman No Cry' was cemented by their singer Lauryn Hill having a child with Marley's son Rohan, while in 1999 Danish DJ and producer Martin Ottesen, operating under the moniker of Funkstar de Luxe, took 'Sun Is Shining' into the UK Top 3. It's certain that many who bought the 'updated' version, a new dancefloor-orientated beat behind Bob's vocal in place of the original sparse, melodica-laced backing, had not even been born when Marley was in his prime.

GENRES

Reggae

ACTIVE YEARS

1963–81

CLASSIC RECORDINGS

Catch A Fire, 'Stir It Up', 'I Shot The Sheriff', *Live!*, 'No Woman, No Cry', *Exodus*, *Kaya*, *Survival*, *Uprising*, 'Could You Be Loved'

METALLICA

VOCAL/INSTRUMENTAL GROUP

Formed in California in 1981 by drummer Lars Ulrich and James Hetfield (vocals, guitar) who shared a mutual love of British new-wave heavy metal, Metallica were completed by Dave Mustaine (lead guitar) and Ron McGovney (bass). Due to personal and musical issues the pair were quickly replaced by Kirk Hammett (lead guitar) and Cliff Burton (bass). After two albums for the Megaforce label the band signed an eight-album deal with Elektra Records. *Master Of Puppets* (1986) became Metallica's first fully fledged masterpiece and remains one of the best extreme metal albums ever recorded. However, tragedy struck during a 1986 European tour when the band's bus overturned killing Burton. Jason Newsted soon slotted into the live and studio machine.

Metallica (1991) was another career landmark and saw the quartet embrace the previously resisted music-video market for the first time on songs like 'Enter Sandman' and 'Nothing Else Matters'. Metallica won nine Grammy Awards and had five consecutive albums debut at No. 1 on the *Billboard* 200, the first band to do so. Metallica remain culturally significant: they appeared in *The Simpsons* (2006) and have sold an estimated 100 million records worldwide. In 2008 they released their ninth album *Death Magnetic*.

GENRES

Heavy Metal, Thrash Metal

ACTIVE YEARS

1981–present

CLASSIC RECORDINGS

Kill 'Em All, Ride The Lightning, Master Of Puppets, ...And Justice For All, 'One', *Metallica,* 'Enter Sandman', *Load,* 'Until It Sleeps', *ReLoad*

JONI MITCHELL
GUITAR, VOCALS

Fairport Convention were among several artists who had already covered Joni Mitchell's songs when this gifted Canadian soprano's debut LP, *Songs To A Seagull*, appeared in 1968. A move to California coupled with relentless touring assisted the passage of the following year's *Clouds* into the US Top 40. However, it was not until she caught the general tenor of the post–Woodstock era that Mitchell truly left the runway with 1970's *Ladies Of The Canyon* and its spin-off hit single, 'Big Yellow Taxi'. Another song from the album, 'Woodstock', was covered by Matthews' Southern Comfort and the single shot to No. 1 in Britain in October of that year.

Blue (1971) and *Court And Spark* (1974) – Mitchell's first album with all-amplified accompaniment – were particularly big sellers before a jazzier approach in the later 1970s was received less enthusiastically. Since then, artistic and commercial progress has been patchy and has involved ventures into other cultural areas – most conspicuously exhibitions of her paintings in the mid-1990s – and increasingly longer periods of vanishing from the public eye. In 2007 she released *Shine*, her first album of new songs in nine years, through the Starbucks coffee-house chain's label Hear Music. In 2010 Mitchell, a childhood polio victim, revealed she was suffering from Morgellons syndrome and planned to leave the music industry to raise awareness of the disease.

GENRES

Folk Rock, Jazz

ACTIVE YEARS

1964–present

CLASSIC RECORDINGS

Song To A Seagull, *Clouds*, *Ladies Of The Canyon*, 'Big Yellow Taxi', *Blue*, *Court And Spark*, 'Help Me', 'Free Man In Paris', *Hejira*

THE MOODY BLUES

VOCAL/INSTRUMENTAL GROUP

Though 'Go Now' was a worldwide smash in 1965, later singles were much less successful for The Moody Blues. The original line-up of Denny Laine (vocals, guitar), Mike Pinder (keyboards), Ray Thomas, (woodwinds, percussion), Clint Warwick (bass) and Graeme Edge (drums) were all veterans of several beat groups from the British Midlands. But with the departures of the late Warwick and Laine (later in Paul McCartney's Wings), the group were sagging on the ropes by 1967. However, with the respective enlistments of John Lodge and Justin Hayward, they revived with 'Nights In White Satin', the hit single from *Days Of Future Passed* (1967), an ambitious concept LP featuring an orchestra. Consequent albums refined a grandiose style so nebulous in scope that such diverse units as Yes, King Crimson and Roxy Music were all cited erroneously as variants of The Moody Blues prototype.

Following a sabbatical for solo projects in the mid-1970s, the group reassembled for 1978's *Octave* and further albums that have tended to sell steadily if unremarkably in Britain. In the States it's another matter: *The Other Side Of Life* was a 1986 album that took the band back to the US Top 10 after a five-year absence, while predecessor *Long Distance Voyager* (1981) was a US chart-topper. Ray Thomas retired from the band in 2003. His warm baritone, inspired flute-playing and intense tambourine-thrashing were much missed.

GENRES

Progressive Rock, Symphonic Rock

ACTIVE YEARS

1964–74, 1977–present

CLASSIC RECORDINGS

'Go Now', *Days Of Future Passed*, 'Nights In White Satin', *On The Threshold Of A Dream*, *A Question Of Balance*, *Octave*, *Long Distance Voyager*

VAN MORRISON

VOCALS

After leaving Irish beat group Them, Van Morrison relocated to the States in 1967 to launch a solo career. Debut single 'Brown Eyed Girl' was a hit in America but not Britain, while second album *Astral Weeks* (1968) was a massively influential work, which added Celtic and jazz influences to his R&B and soul roots. Based initially in Boston and then California, Morrison produced a string of albums including *Moondance* (1970), *Tupelo Honey* (1971) and *St Dominic's Preview* (1972) while touring extensively with the Caledonia Soul Orchestra. His 1974 live set, *It's Too Late To Stop Now*, marked the end of this prolific early phase as Van returned to Ireland to explore his Celtic roots.

The theme of spiritual quest came to prominence in the albums he made in the 1980s. In 1988 he revisited his roots with The Chieftains on *Irish Heartbeat*, while 1989's *Avalon Sunset* was his most commercially successful for many years. In 1999 Morrison released *Back On Top*, which spawned his first solo UK Top 40 hit with the single 'Precious Time', while 2000 saw him unite with the musical heroes of his youth, skiffle maestro Lonnie Donegan and jazzman Chris Barber, on stage at Belfast's Whitla Hall. His career continues its idiosyncratic path today.

GENRES

R&B, Soul, Celtic, Jazz, Blues

ACTIVE YEARS

1967–present

CLASSIC RECORDINGS

'Brown Eyed Girl', *Astral Weeks*, *Moondance*, 'Domino', *Tupelo Honey*, 'Wild Night', *It's Too Late To Stop Now*, *Avalon Sunset*, *Back On Top*

MUDDY WATERS

GUITAR, VOCALS

Born McKinley Morganfield in Mississippi, Muddy Waters experienced all the poverty of the rural South. Sent to his grandmother's at the age of three, he picked up his stage name because she used to say he sneaked out and played in the mud. He was first recorded by musicologist Alan Lomax, and 'I Be's Troubled' would become Waters' first hit when he recorded it in Chicago as 'I Can't Be Satisfied' (1948). By 1951, Waters was on the R&B charts consistently with tunes like 'Louisiana Blues' and 'Long Distance Call'. In 1952, he created the smash 'She Moves Me', and later came 'I'm Your Hoochie Coochie Man' and 'I'm Ready'. Bo Diddley borrowed a Waters beat for 'I'm A Man' in 1955, and then Waters reworked the idea into 'Mannish Boy'. In 1956, Waters had three more R&B smashes.

Waters' tour of 1958 almost single-handedly turned Britain onto the blues. The fact he was playing an amplified guitar shocked the purists, but inspired Alexis Korner and Cyril Davies to form Blues Incorporated, not to mention followers like The Rolling Stones (named after a Waters tune) and Eric Clapton. He'd enjoy a Grammy-winning comeback two decades later courtesy of Johnny Winter, another long-time fan, and continued performing and releasing albums until his death in 1983.

GENRES

Chicago Blues, Electric Blues

ACTIVE YEARS

1941–82

CLASSIC RECORDINGS

'I Can't Be Satisfied', 'Louisiana Blues', 'Long Distance Call', 'She Moves Me', 'I'm Your Hoochie Coochie Man', 'I'm Ready'

TOP 100
ROCK ARTISTS

NIRVANA

VOCAL/INSTRUMENTAL GROUP

One of the most influential acts of the 1990s, Nirvana split the rock world as no other band: love or hate, there was no in-between. Like James Marshall Hendrix, another left-handed guitar legend from Seattle, frontman Kurt Cobain would blaze briefly but brightly, leaving an enduring influence far in excess of his back catalogue.

Nirvana was formed in Aberdeen, Washington, in 1987 by Cobain (guitar, vocals) and Krist Novoselic (bass), with Chad Channing (drums) cementing the band's early line-up. For the first seven years of his life, Cobain listened to nothing but The Beatles. To find out how the music of Nirvana could blend the sweetest of melodies with all that pent-up aggression, look no further than *Abbey Road* (1969). Signed by Seattle's growing Sub Pop label, their first single was a cover version of The Shocking Blue's 'Love Bug' with sole songwriter Cobain penning 'Big Cheese' on the B-side. The initial pressing was limited to 1,000 copies.

EARLY ACCLAIM

Over the next year, Nirvana appeared on various compilations and briefly became a four-piece when Jason Everman (guitar) was drafted in for live work. Everman paid the $600 recording fee for Nirvana's first Sub Pop album *Bleach* (1989). Although pictured on the cover, he did not play on the record. Released in June 1989 the bedrock of the Nirvana sound was evident, the melodic beauty of 'About A Girl' contrasting with the loud, aggressive punk metal of 'Swap Meet' and 'Paper Cuts'. With hand-to-mouth American and European touring, Nirvana began to receive critical acclaim with Cobain keen to stress the influence of The Pixies on the Nirvana sound. (A second UK tour planned for the spring of 1990 was cancelled when Channing departed.) Nirvana's guitarist, lead singer and songwriter had the ability to write songs that combined urgency and noise with incredibly catchy melodies, played in a loose, almost jamming style. Cobain once said

in an interview with French television: 'Punk rock should mean freedom. It means playing whatever you want as sloppy as you want as long as it's good and has passion.'

THE NEVERMIND EFFECT

Nirvana's second Sub Pop single – 'Sliver'/'Dive' – was followed by the recruitment of experienced drummer David Grohl who had toured and recorded with hardcore act Scream. Courted and signed by Geffen, Nirvana set about recording a second album with producer Butch Vig. Geffen were taken by surprise when initial pressing of 50,000 copies of *Nevermind* (1991) sold out in two days. By now, generational anthem 'Smells Like Teen Spirit' had been released and became Nirvana's first Top 10 single in the US and the UK. The song's typically obscure title, which didn't occur in its lyrics was inspired by Cobain's hometown Aberdeen, where it had been a spray-painted graffiti on the wall. The follow up 'Come As You Are' cemented Nirvana as the most celebrated new band in the world and the multi-platinum *Nevermind* became one of the most important and influential albums of the decade.

For Cobain, success was a double-edged sword as, like Bob Dylan before him, he was now perceived as the spokesman of a generation – and the entire Seattle-inspired 'grunge' movement. Touring *Nevermind* around the world Cobain tired of 'Teen Spirit', improvising new lyrics and appeared on UK TV's *Top of The Pops* delivering the vocal as if sung by former Smiths lead singer Morrissey. Reacting against the commercial sheen of *Nevermind*, sessions for the next album were recorded mostly live in two weeks with producer Steve Albini, formerly of the thunderous Big Black.

IN UTERO

Despite record company objection to the raw sound and pressure that led to the remixing of two tracks, 'Pennyroyal Tea' and 'Dumb', by R.E.M. producer Scott Litt, *In Utero* was released as the band intended and topped the charts on both sides of the Atlantic in 1993. Away from music, Cobain married Hole singer Courtney Love in February 1992 who gave birth to their daughter Frances Bean six months later. By 1993, Cobain and Love were addicted to heroin, a chemical romance that was, in part, played out in public with state threats to remove the child from their care.

In November 1993, Nirvana demonstrated on a live *MTV Unplugged* session that their loud guitar-based songs could be distilled into acoustic beauty. Cobain's state of mind grew darker and, after failing with one suicide attempt in March 1994 during a European tour, he shot himself with a rifle at his Seattle home on 8 April 1994. Like Joy Division lead singer Ian Curtis, it was only after his suicide that songs like 'I Hate Myself And Want To Die' were judged to be Cobain's state of mind rather than mere lyrics.

A LASTING LEGACY

Cobain left a wife, a daughter and a personal legacy that, today, has expanded into iconic proportions. The publication of portions of his journals, a slew of biographies, films, albums, documentaries and even a comic-book graphic novel continue to stoke and expand the legend. *Rolling Stone* magazine caused controversy when it rated the by-then departed Kurt Cobain No. 12 in a poll of 100 great guitar players, beating the immortal quartet of Van Halen, May, Beck and Gilmour – surely thanks to his effect and influence rather than his technique.

Post-Nirvana, Grohl, now singing and playing guitar, formed the successful Foo Fighters. Novoselic has chosen to keep a lower profile and has dabbled in politics.

GENRES

Grunge, Alternative Rock

ACTIVE YEARS

1987–94

CLASSIC RECORDINGS

Nevermind, 'Smells Like Teen Spirit', 'Come As You Are', 'Lithium', *Incesticide*, *In Utero*, 'Heart-Shaped Box', *MTV Unplugged In New York*

OASIS

VOCAL/INSTRUMENTAL GROUP

Mancunian brothers Liam (vocals) and Noel (guitar) Gallagher, Paul 'Bonehead' Arthurs (guitar), Paul 'Guigsy' McGuigan (bass) and Tony McCarroll (drums) signed to Creation Records in 1993 as Oasis. The band's updated take on The Beatles' sound put them in the 'Britpop' category, vying for supremacy with Blur's Kinks-inspired southern whimsy.

Debut single 'Supersonic' (1994) was a melodic, guitar-driven tune over which Liam snarled out lyrics. By the end of the year another four singles – all instant classics – had graced the charts. Meanwhile, debut album *Definitely Maybe* (1994) began a run of 174 weeks in the album charts. Aside from Noel's perfectly constructed pop songs dominated by memorable choruses, the feuding between the two brothers delighted tabloid editors. This friction did not affect the music with *(What's The Story) Morning Glory?* (1995) going on to become the second biggest-selling UK album of all time. Songs like 'Champagne Supernova' and especially 'Wonderwall' would never be surpassed. In America *Morning Glory* and 'Wonderwall' went Top 10, a breakthrough no Britpop band could match. Stadium tours of the UK became obligatory and *Be Here Now* (1997) kept the hits coming, for a while at least. Despite personnel changes Liam and Noel buried their differences until a very public 2009 split.

GENRES

Britpop, Alternative Rock

ACTIVE YEARS

1991–2009

CLASSIC RECORDINGS

Definitely Maybe, (What's The Story) Morning Glory?, 'Some Might Say', 'Wonderwall', 'Don't Look Back In Anger', *Be Here Now, Heathen Chemistry*

TOP 100
ROCK ARTISTS

PARLIAMENT-FUNKADELIC

VOCAL/INSTRUMENTAL GROUP

Born in North Carolina and raised in New Jersey, George Clinton became a funk legend. His first musical venture was the five-man doo-wop group The Parliaments formed in the late 1950s. After recording for various small labels, and following a spell working for Motown, signs of Clinton's future direction appeared on The Parliaments' 1967 American Top 20 single '(I Wanna) Testify'. Contractual difficulties over the group's name prompted Clinton to record with The Parliaments' backing band, newly christened Funkadelic to reflect their psychedelic side. Clinton then set up the collective of musicians that operated under the banner of Parliament-Funkadelic in the 1970s.

Onstage, as lead singer of Parliament, Clinton was a consummate showman indulging his penchant for bizarre costumes. Clinton's best-known song is Funkadelic's 'One Nation Under A Groove', a Top 10 UK hit in 1979. He launched a solo career in 1981. Few musicians have proved as influential on all areas of music: Clinton produced white rockers Red Hot Chili Peppers' 1985 album *Freakey Styley*, collaborated with Primal Scream a decade later and has worked with hip-hop artists like Tupac Shakur, Redman and the Wu Tang Clan. Alongside James Brown, Clinton is considered to be one of the most-sampled musicians ever.

GENRES

Funk, Soul, Psychedelic Rock

ACTIVE YEARS

1968–81

CLASSIC RECORDINGS

Funkadelic, *Free Your Mind... And Your Ass Will Follow*, *Maggot Brain*, *One Nation Under A Groove*, 'One Nation Under A Groove', *Uncle Jam Wants You*

PEARL JAM

VOCAL/INSTRUMENTAL GROUP

Emerging out of former Seattle band Mother Love Bone, the classic Pearl Jam line-up consisted of Eddie Vedder (vocals), Stone Gossard (guitar), Mike McCready (guitar), Jeff Ament (bass) and Dave Abbruzzese (drums). The spiky hook-laden rock of *Ten* (1991) sold in large numbers after Nirvana made Seattle alternative bands popular. Touring with the Lollapalooza II circus cemented Pearl Jam's position as major players.

A refusal to record promotional videos, release singles or tour, did not prevent their second album *Vs* (1993) going platinum. *Vitalogy* (1994) confirmed their position as one of the biggest bands in America, but rather than plough one musical furrow, on subsequent albums like *No Code* (1996) Pearl Jam vastly expanded their musical references to include folk and even world music. In an effort to defeat bootleggers they released 25 double live albums in 2002. Five of these albums clambered into the US charts, confirming longevity and long-term appeal. An eponymous 2006 album, their first for J Records, was recorded live in the studio, recapturing their early sound, while ninth studio album *Backspacer* (2009) was a homage to the new wave. Vedder and band continue to show a social conscience, playing a gig for Hurricane Katrina victims in 2005 and speaking out against the war in Iraq. The band continue to tour.

GENRES

Grunge, Alternative Rock

ACTIVE YEARS

1990–present

CLASSIC RECORDINGS

Ten, 'Jeremy', *Vs*, *Vitalogy*, *No Code*, *Yield*, 'Given To Fly', 'Last Kiss', *Pearl Jam*, *Backspacer*

TOM PETTY

GUITAR, SINGER/SONGWRITER

Petty, born in Gainsville, Florida, formed his long-time backing band The Heartbreakers from Mike Campbell (guitar), Benmont Tench (keyboards), Ron Blair (bass) and Stan Lynch (drums). An eponymous album in 1977 was a hard-hitting brand of country rock, with plenty of modern attack, rootsy authenticity and good tunes. The UK was impressed, but it was not until 1979's *Damn The Torpedoes* that the US took a native son (and another 'new Dylan') to its breast. Alongside Springsteen, Petty helped revitalize the reputation of intelligent blue-collar rock, while tapping into its folkier heritage. Tom Petty & The Heartbreakers scored a couple of big US singles in 'Refugee' (1979) and 'Don't Do Me Like That' (1980). Petty meanwhile took on his record company, refusing to be transferred when his label was sold, even filing for bankruptcy before the dispute was resolved. He has since insisted on retaining creative control.

In 1988, Petty wound-up the band, working with Bob Dylan, Roy Orbison and George Harrison in The Travelling Wilburys. He made an excellent solo album, *Full Moon Fever*, in 1989, before The Heartbreakers reformed. They are still one of America's most consistent bands and Petty remains a consistently good songwriter. Petty has branched out into acting and related works and was a regular on animated TV show *King Of The Hill*.

GENRES

Country Rock, Folk Rock

ACTIVE YEARS

1976–present

CLASSIC RECORDINGS

Damn The Torpedoes, 'Don't Do Me Like That', 'Refugee', *Hard Promises, Southern Accents, Full Moon Fever, Into The Great Wide Open*

PINK FLOYD

VOCAL/INSTRUMENTAL GROUP

Pink Floyd, the biggest progressive rock band of the 1970s, were formed in London in 1965 by singer/guitarist Syd Barrett, bassist Roger Waters, keyboard player Richard Wright and drummer Nick Mason. Barrett and Waters had grown up together in Cambridge before moving to London. Playing a mixture of R&B (their name came from an amalgam of blues artists Pink Anderson and Floyd Council) and primitive electronic music enhanced by a psychedelic light show, they became a big underground attraction.

Two quirky singles written by Barrett, 'Arnold Layne' and 'See Emily Play', made the chart. Barrett also wrote the songs on their debut album, *Piper At The Gates Of Dawn* (1967), which made No. 6, combining a nursery rhyme musical sensibility with LSD–inspired imagery. By the end of 1967, however, Barrett's increasingly unstable behaviour was becoming a liability, and at the beginning of 1968 the band drafted in David Gilmour as additional guitarist. Barrett left in March and went into seclusion, emerging in 1970 to record idiosyncratic solo albums *The Madcap Laughs* and *Barrett* before retiring from music.

A NEW CHAPTER

Pink Floyd's second album *A Saucerful Of Secrets* (1968) was dominated by longer, more ambitious numbers like 'Set The Controls For The Heart Of The Sun' and led them to write the soundtrack for the film *More* (1969). *Ummagumma* (1969) was a double album with idiosyncratic individual pieces and live tracks. It reached No. 5 but there was a lack of direction. *Atom Heart Mother* (1970) restored their credibility. The side–long title track was a classical–rock fusion with an orchestra and choir and laid the seeds for the band's future direction. It gave them their first UK No. 1 album.

On *Meddle* (1971) Pink Floyd expanded their sound and dynamics on the 23–minute 'Echoes' that linked a series of riffs into an epic masterpiece and the menacing 'One Of These Days'. The album peaked at No. 3.

Pink Floyd spent several months working on their next album, *Dark Side Of The Moon* (1973). It proved to be a ground-breaking concept album themed around the pressures of modern life, paranoia and schizophrenia. It caught the zeitgeist but its appeal remains timeless. In the UK it got to No. 2 and spent six years in the charts. In the US it was Pink Floyd's first hit album and spent one week at No. 1. Worldwide sales of *Dark Side Of The Moon* are now over 30 million and rising.

Wish You Were Here (1975) explored similar themes of madness and alienation. The 26-minute 'Shine On You Crazy Diamond' was a tribute to Barrett. By now Waters was dominant and the next album, *Animals* (1977), was a bleak, Orwellian view of the world lightened by the acoustic, two-part 'Pigs On The Wing'. Live shows featured quadraphonic sound, lights, film, animation and inflatable pigs hovering above the audience. In contrast, the band were deliberately anonymous.

ON TOP OF THE WALL

Pink Floyd's next album was Waters' most ambitious concept. *The Wall* (1979) was a dense double album that dealt with the barriers created by society and individuals. 'Another Brick In The Wall Part 2', an anti-education rant, was a rare but successful single, topping the US charts for four weeks and becoming a UK No. 1. *The Wall* spent 15 weeks at the top of the US album charts. Pink Floyd constructed a giant wall across the stage between themselves and the audience and played behind it until the wall tumbled down. In 1982 it was turned into a movie.

Wright was fired during the making of *The Wall* album but was re-hired for the concerts. And Gilmour and Mason had little input into the next Pink Floyd album, *The Final Cut* (1983), a caustic, heartfelt diatribe by Waters on the futility of war. Although the album went to No. 1 in the UK (*The Wall* had only reached No. 3), it peaked at No. 6 in the US and sold less than previous albums. In 1984 Gilmour released a solo album, *About Face*, and played a low-key tour while Waters released *The Pros And Cons Of Hitch-Hiking* (1984) and embarked on an arena tour of Europe and America.

In 1986 Waters left Pink Floyd and a legal battle then ensued over rights to the name. The next Pink Floyd album, *A Momentary Lapse Of Reason* (1987), restored Wright alongside Gilmour and Mason and made No. 3 in the UK and US.

The band played a stadium tour of America and Europe, captured on *Delicate Sound Of Thunder* (1987), which got to No. 11 in the US and UK. Waters, meanwhile, released *Radio KAOS* (1987) and *Amused To Death* (1992). He also staged a production of *The Wall* on the site of the recently demolished Berlin Wall in 1990.

LAVISH LIVE SHOWS

Pink Floyd returned in 1994 with *The Division Bell*, another No. 1 album in the US and UK. The subsequent tour was lavish, even by Pink Floyd standards, and included a complete performance of *Dark Side Of The Moon*. It was seen by over five million people and documented on the live *Pulse* (1995) – also No. 1 in the US and UK. After the tour, Pink Floyd wound down. Gilmour began recording an album, the UK chart-topping *On An Island* released in 2006. Waters meanwhile undertook an 'In The Flesh' world tour in 2002 and worked on an opera, *Ca Ira* (2005).

It was a considerable surprise in June 2005 when Bob Geldof announced that Waters, Gilmour, Wright and Mason would be appearing at the Live 8 Festival in London. They played a 25-minute set and dedicated 'Wish You Were Here' to their founder and mentor Syd Barrett. A year later Barrett died from complications arising from diabetes. Rick Wright later died in 2008 after a battle with cancer.

GENRES

Psychedelic Rock, Progressive Rock

ACTIVE YEARS

1965–94

CLASSIC RECORDINGS

'Arnold Layne', *The Dark Side Of The Moon*, *Wish You Were Here*, *Animals*, *The Wall*, 'Another Brick In The Wall, Part II', *The Division Bell*

THE POLICE

VOCAL/INSTRUMENTAL GROUP

One of the most successful British bands of the 1980s, The Police were founded in London at the height of the punk boom in 1977. Former Curved Air drummer Stewart Copeland joined singer/bassist Sting (born Gordon Sumner) and guitarist Henri Padovani. After independent single 'Fall Out' they were joined by veteran guitarist Andy Summers, formerly of Dantalian's Chariot and Eric Burdon's New Animals.

Padovani departed and the remaining threesome developed a unique, almost minimalist sound in the blend of Summers' crisp guitar, Sting's distinctive voice and Copeland's clattering drums. Heavily influenced by reggae, their first two singles 'Roxanne' and 'Can't Stand Losing You' did not chart when first released in 1978 – the BBC took a dim view of prostitution and suicide as subject matter. The belated success of the reactivated singles ('Roxanne' also became a Top 30 hit in America) launched the debut album *Outlandos D'Amour* (1978) into the UK chart.

NEW WAVE SUCCESS

Reggatta De Blanc (1979) quickly followed and went to No. 1 in Britain, along with the first two singles lifted from it, 'Message In A Bottle' and 'Walking On The Moon', confirming The Police as the country's most popular new group. Mainstream success in America arrived when *Zenyatta Mondatta* (1980) went Top 5 and spawned two US Top 10 singles, 'Don't Stand So Close To Me' (another UK chart topper) and 'De Do Do Do, De Da Da Da'. Recorded in the midst of touring commitments, the band were dissatisfied with the album and the critical reception was lukewarm.

The lead single from *Ghost In The Machine* (1981), 'Invisible Sun', referred to Northern Ireland and was a brave departure for the band. The album featured a more expansive sound, utilizing saxophones and synthesizer, with more thoughtful lyrics to match, something not reflected in the infectious No. 1 'Every Little Thing She Does Is Magic'.

Summers, Copeland and Sting took a year out for solo projects in 1982, reconvening to record *Synchronicity* (1983). By this time, tensions, particularly between Sting and Copeland were threatening to tear the band apart. Nevertheless, The Police managed to produce their biggest-selling album, spending 17 weeks on top of the American chart. The first of four singles to be taken from *Synchronicity* was the classic, subtly sinister 'Every Breath You Take', an international chart topper. 'Wrapped Around Your Finger' followed it into the Top 10.

THE INEVITABLE SPLIT

The Police played their final shows in Melbourne, Australia in March 1984 at the end of the *Synchronicity* world tour. There was no official announcement that the band had split up, although Sting was quick to launch his solo career. The Police have reconvened occasionally since, playing three dates on the Amnesty International Conspiracy of Hope tour in 1986, which led to re-recordings of 'De Do Do Do, De Da Da Da' and 'Don't Stand So Close To Me'. In 1992, they played together at Sting's wedding and, in March 2003, performed three numbers to celebrate their induction into the Rock And Roll Hall Of Fame. They re-formed in 2007 to celebrate their thirtieth anniversary with a world tour.

One of rock's high-profile stars, Sting's solo work has been predictably successful, starting with the jazzy *Dream Of The Blue Turtles* (1985) through the loose concept album *Ten Summoner's Tales* (1993) to his twenty-first-century output. He has also been a high-profile campaigner for the Rainforest Foundation.

GENRES

Rock, New Wave, Jazz, Reggae

ACTIVE YEARS

1977–84, 1986, 2007–08

CLASSIC RECORDINGS

Outlandos D'Amour, 'Message In A Bottle', 'Don't Stand So Close To Me', 'Every Little Thing She Does Is Magic', *Synchronicity*, 'Every Breath You Take'

ELVIS PRESLEY

VOCALS, GUITAR

Elvis Aaron Presley was born in his family's shot–gun shack in Tupelo, Mississippi. His twin brother died at birth and his mother doted on her sole son. Elvis loved to sing at the local First Assembly of God church. His mother, Gladys, and father, Vernon, moved to Memphis when Elvis was 13. Throughout his adolescence, Elvis would drink in music of every variety, from Dean Martin to Arthur 'Big Boy' Crudup, from The Blackwood Brothers Quartet to Mario Lanza.

Presley graduated from Humes High School and, in summer 1953, presented himself at Sun studios at 706 Union Avenue to record 'My Happiness' and 'That's When Your Heartaches Begin' for his mother. Unsuccessful, he returned in January 1954, and secretary Marion Keisker suggested studio boss Sam Phillips give him a try. Phillips put him together with guitarist Scotty Moore and Bill Black, a bassist and natural clown.

A WINNING COMBINATION

Their session on 5 July 1954 seemed to be going nowhere until Elvis started messing around on an old Arthur Crudup blues, 'That's All Right', attacking it with vigour. Phillips knew that this was the combination of country and blues, sung by a charismatic young white man, he had been searching for. A hopped–up version of Bill Monroe's bluegrass classic 'Blue Moon Of Kentucky' completed the single, rush–released as Sun 209 on 17 July 1954. It lit up the Memphis area.

Four more Sun records followed the same blueprint. 'I Forgot To Remember To Forget', the flip side to the awesome blues power of 'Mystery Train' – the final Sun single – even made the Top 10 of the national country charts. Colonel Tom Parker, who looked after country star Hank Snow, became Presley's manager, and Elvis's contract with Sun was sold on to RCA in late 1955 for $35,000 – a very large amount of money for a struggling concern.

Elvis went into RCA's Nashville Studios on 10 January 1956, two days after he turned 21. Black and Moore were there with him, alongside session-men Floyd Cramer on piano and guitarist Chet Atkins. Presley was unfazed and laid down 'Heartbreak Hotel', which became his first No. 1, and several tracks for his self-titled first album.

HITS GALORE

In the singles charts, 'I Want You, I Need You, I Love You', 'Hound Dog', 'Too Much' and 'All Shook Up' all went to the US No. 1 slot within a year and a half of his RCA debut. There was also 'Love Me Tender' (1956) from the film of the same name and '(Let Me Be Your) Teddy Bear' from *Loving You* (1957), his first two movies. He completed a celluloid quartet, with *Jailhouse Rock* (1957) and *King Creole* (1958), before he was drafted into the US Army.

While serving in Germany, Elvis suffered the loss of his beloved mother. When he was demobbed in March 1960, he seemed to have grown-up, but that was not all to the good. Great tracks still emerged – 'Mess Of Blues' (1960), 'Return To Sender' (1962) – but they were outnumbered by the tracks from the often awful films he made. In May 1967, he married Priscilla Beaulieu, and in February 1968, their daughter Lisa Marie was born.

THE COMEBACK SPECIAL

Elvis was not happy with his career at this point and neither were his public. His return to form can be traced to his gospel album, *How Great Thou Art* (1967), which reached back to his roots, and the superb 'Guitar Man' (1968). It was the June TV show, known as the 1968 *Comeback Special*, however, that relaunched his career. Dressed in black leather and reunited with Scotty Moore, he seemed on top of his game, running through gems from his back catalogue with fervour.

Elvis moved straight on to some of his finest recorded work at producer Chip Moman's American studio in Memphis. *From Elvis In Memphis* (1969) yielded the surprisingly political 'In The Ghetto'. The glorious 'Suspicious Minds' (1969) then gave him his first No. 1 for over four years.

TOP 100
ROCK ARTISTS

Presley returned to regular live performance, first at the International Hotel in Las Vegas, where he opened an incredibly successful season of shows on 31 July 1969. This period was captured on the documentary, *Elvis: That's The Way It Is* (1970); the live satellite broadcast, *Aloha From Hawaii* (1973); and on the album, *Elvis: As Recorded At Madison Square Garden* (1972).

MOUNTING PROBLEMS

Priscilla left the Presley home Graceland in late 1971, and it affected Elvis badly. His consumption of prescription drugs increased massively, and his prolific live shows often suffered. He had financial worries as well as personal ones, and so had to keep on the touring treadmill. Presley had his last Top 20 US hit – before the posthumous triumph of 'Way Down' – with 'Promised Land' in late 1974. He was admitted to hospital at least three times in 1975, the year that also marked his last session in a recording studio. From then on he laid down his tracks at Graceland, taping a final pair of shows for a CBS *Elvis In Concert* special in June 1977. His drug–ravaged body, however, had had enough, and on 16 August 1977 he died of heart failure.

Elvis was the first and ultimate rock star, as well as playing a massive part in creating the 'rock' that he was 'star' of. He was the most charismatic performer in popular music history and one of the most talented; and his latest No. 1, a 2005 remix of 1968's 'A Little Less Conversation', proves that, at least musically, he still lives.

GENRES

Rock'n'Roll, Rockabilly

ACTIVE YEARS

1954–77

CLASSIC RECORDINGS

'Heartbreak Hotel', *Elvis*, 'All Shook Up', 'Jailhouse Rock', *Elvis Is Back!*, *From Elvis In Memphis*, 'In The Ghetto', 'Suspicious Minds'

PRINCE

GUITAR, VOCALS

The most innovative, mercurial and controversial black rock star since Jimi Hendrix, Prince (born Prince Rogers Nelson) is also one of the most mysterious. His father was the leader of a local jazz band, his mother was a singer. He formed his first band at 14 and signed a self-production deal with Warner Brothers in 1977.

His debut, *For You* (1978), was almost entirely self-written and self-played. *Prince* (1979) peaked just outside the US Top 20; one track from the album, 'I Feel For You', would later be a major hit for Chaka Khan. Prince then toured America, supporting and outshining Rick James. *Dirty Mind* (1980) was loosely conceptual and included provocative songs like 'Head' and 'Sister', but proved less successful. *Controversy* (1981) refined his adult-oriented funk and revived his fortunes. His breakthrough came with double album *1999* (1982) that hit the US Top 10 on the back of three Top 10 singles: 'Little Red Corvette', 'Delirious' and the title track. But it was *Purple Rain* (1984) that vaulted Prince to superstardom, topping the US charts for 24 weeks. The soundtrack to an autobiographical movie, it featured two US No. 1 hits – 'When Doves Cry' and 'Let's Go Crazy'.

SOUNDTRACK OF THE TIMES

Eschewing media interviews and promotion, Prince's image rested on his albums, videos and shows. He released the spiritually inclined *Around The World In A Day* (1985) that topped the US charts for three weeks and made the UK Top 5. Next album *Parade* (1986), his eighth in as many years, went Top 5 in the US and UK and featured songs from his second movie, *Under The Cherry Moon* (1986), including the US No. 1 (and UK No. 4) 'Kiss'. Double album *Sign 'O' The Times* (1987) was similarly successful, and *Lovesexy* (1988) was the first of three consecutive UK No. 1 albums. *Batman* (1989), the soundtrack to the year's movie blockbuster, was a US and UK No. 1. *Graffiti Bridge* (1990) was another soundtrack,

and a version of the Prince-penned 'Nothing Compares 2 U' by Sinead O'Connor topped the US and UK charts in 1990. Prince scored another US No. 1 with 'Cream' from *Diamonds And Pearls* (1991), which reached No. 3 (No. 2 in the UK).

SYMBOLS AND SELF-INDULGENCE

For *Symbol* (1992), Prince created his own hieroglyph, combining the male and female symbols and scored his fourth UK No. 1 (US No. 6), then changed his name to the unpronounceable symbol. The independently released 'The Most Beautiful Girl In The World' was a No. 1 hit around much of the world in 1994 (US No. 3).

Prince's contract with Warners ended with *Chaos And Disorder* (1996), a US Top 30 and UK Top 20 album. He celebrated his release with the triple CD *Emancipation* (1996), which went Top 20 in the US and UK. Once independent, however, he made little effort to court commercial success. *Rave Un2 The Joy Fantastic* (1999) made the US Top 20 but subsequent albums were increasingly self-indulgent until the focused *Musicology* (2004) made No. 3 in the UK and US.

The album *3121* (2006) gave Prince his first US No. 1 since *Batman* and made the UK Top 10, but he chose to give away 2007 album *Planet Earth* free with a newspaper. He repeated the same tactic with 2010's *20TEN*.

GENRES

Pop, Rock, Funk, R&B

ACTIVE YEARS

1976–present

CLASSIC RECORDINGS

1999, Purple Rain, 'When Doves Cry', 'Purple Rain', 'Kiss', *Sign 'O' The Times,* 'Batdance', *Diamonds And Pearls,* 'The Most Beautiful Girl In The World'

QUEEN

VOCAL/INSTRUMENTAL GROUP

The gorgeously flamboyant Queen were formed in 1970 in London by singer Freddie Mercury (born Farrokh Bulsara), guitarist Brian May and drummer Roger Taylor, with bassist John Deacon completing the line-up in 1971. They spent two years developing their style while they remained at college, playing gigs here and there. Once they started touring after the release of *Queen* (1973), their live performances – and Mercury's extrovert personality – quickly won them a following.

A SONGWRITING QUARTET

Queen II (1974) gave the band their first UK hit with 'Seven Seas Of Rhye' but it was the tight harmonies and dynamic playing of 'Killer Queen' from their third album, *Sheer Heart Attack* (1974), that marked them out from the fading glam rock wave. Queen delivered the *coup de grace* in 1975 with 'Bohemian Rhapsody', a six-minute epic that blended operatic vocals with metal guitars. The single, boosted by a ground-breaking video, stormed the British charts, staying at No. 1 for nine weeks. The equally extravagant album, *A Night At The Opera* (1975), also topped the UK charts and was a big international success. A key track, 'You're My Best Friend', was written by bassist Deacon; all four members were now contributing strong songs.

Such was Queen's popularity that their fifth album *A Day At The Races* (1976) racked up half a million advance orders ahead of its release. It maintained the momentum with the bombastic 'Tie Your Mother Down' and the compressed 'Somebody To Love' – while *News Of The World* (1977) featured two of rock's greatest anthems: 'We Will Rock You' and 'We Are The Champions'. By now Queen concerts were stadium rallies with the audience playing its part, conducted by the ever more flamboyant Mercury. *Live Killers* (1979) caught the full force of Queen's show. It followed the ambitious *Jazz* (1978) that ranged from metal to pop and included the playful 'Fat Bottomed Girls' and the sporty 'Bicycle Race'.

The rockabilly-styled 'Crazy Little Thing Called Love' was the first sight of a new-look Queen, complete with short hair, as the 1970s ended. Queen's British fans sent the single to No. 2. It came from *The Game* (1980), an unashamed pop album and a UK No. 1. It was their biggest US success, topping the charts for five weeks with two No. 1 singles – the aforementioned 'Crazy Little Thing Called Love' and 'Another One Bites The Dust', penned by Deacon and influenced by disco giants Chic.

Greatest Hits (1981), featuring their latest triumph, 'Flash', the theme song to the 1980 movie *Flash Gordon*, was a massive worldwide success, not least in the UK where it stayed in the charts for nearly eight years. The band also toured South America in 1981, opening up the continent as a rock market. However, concerts in apartheid South Africa caused problems when the band found themselves on the United Nations cultural blacklist.

SOLO CAREERS AND COLLABORATIONS

Band members took time out for solo projects before the next Queen album, *Hot Space* (1982), which flirted with disco and funk and featured a collaboration with David Bowie, 'Under Pressure'. *The Works* (1984) catapulted Queen back to the top after a year's break from the spotlight. It was a broader musical sweep embracing synth pop ('Radio Ga Ga'), hard rock ('Hammer To Fall') and pop ('I Want To Break Free'). The following year they were one of the highlights of Live Aid, an event acknowledged in the single 'One Vision'.

A Kind Of Magic (1986) returned Queen to the top of the UK charts after a six-year absence. The single 'Who Wants To Live Forever' mused on mortality and gained further resonance after Freddie Mercury's death in 1991. Queen played a major tour that year, the last they ever played. The band took another sabbatical (Mercury collaborated with opera diva Montserrat Caballe for the melodramatic 'Barcelona') and it was three years before *The Miracle* (1989), which featured 'I Want It All' and 'Breakthru'.

Rumours were already circulating about Mercury's health and the group chose not to tour but returned to the studio to record another album. *Innuendo* (1991) included 'Headlong' and the grandiose 'The Show Must Go On'.

Mercury continued to deny increasing speculation on his health until November 1991 when he announced that he had AIDS. Two days later, on 24 November, he died at his London home.

CARRYING ON

In April 1992, the remaining Queen members staged A Concert For Life at London's Wembley Stadium, joined by Elton John, George Michael, David Bowie, Guns N' Roses, Metallica and Spinal Tap. That year Queen's iconic status became assured when 'Bohemian Rhapsody' was memorably featured in the *Wayne's World* movie. *Made In Heaven* (1995) was an album of songs recorded with Mercury shortly before he died. It debuted at No. 1 and became Queen's best-selling studio album.

Brian May's bombastic 'We Will Rock You' was revived to chart-topping effect by boy band Five in 2000, with a little help from May and Taylor. It also became the title of a 'jukebox musical' featuring 32 Queen favourites, which was written by Ben Elton and premiered in London's West End in 2002. *We Will Rock You* is set in a nightmare future where listening to rock music and playing guitar is forbidden, the only music around is computer-generated and stars of the calibre of Freddie Mercury do not exist.

Periodically, the remaining group members revive the band for a project. In 2005 and 2006 they toured with former Free and Bad Company vocalist Paul Rogers. Freddie will never really be replaced.

GENRES

Hard Rock, Progressive Rock, Glam Rock, Pop

ACTIVE YEARS

1971–present

CLASSIC RECORDINGS

A Night At The Opera, 'Bohemian Rhapsody', 'We Are The Champions', *The Game*, 'Another One Bites The Dust', 'Radio Ga Ga', *A Kind Of Magic*

TOP 100
ROCK ARTISTS

RADIOHEAD

VOCAL/INSTRUMENTAL GROUP

The five members of Oxford–based Radiohead are the same today as they were the day they formed. Thom Yorke (vocals, guitar, piano), Jonny Greenwood (lead guitar), Ed O'Brien (guitar, vocals), Phil Selway (drums) and Colin Greenwood (bass) met at school in Oxfordshire and started jamming around 1986.

Debut album *Pablo Honey* (1993) contained 'Creep', a slab of neo–12–bar blues, thrillingly 'messed up' by Greenwood, which became a sleeper US hit via college radio. The band's third release, *OK Computer* (1997), was lauded as the greatest album of the year in many publications. The electronic–based *Kid A* (2000) and *Amnesiac* (2001) were made up of works from the same sessions, but released as two separate albums and alienated many original followers. By 2007, Radiohead had fulfilled their EMI recording contract and released album *In Rainbows* on the Internet, allowing fans to pay what they thought it was worth. It later appeared in physical form to critical acclaim and chart success, debuting at No. 1 both in the UK and in the US. Its success proved that Radiohead were still one of the world's most popular and challenging bands.

GENRES

Alternative Rock, Experimental Rock

ACTIVE YEARS

1986–present

CLASSIC RECORDINGS

Pablo Honey, 'Creep', *The Bends*, *OK Computer*, 'Paranoid Android', *Kid A*, *Amnesiac*, 'Pyramid Song', *Hail To The Thief*, 'There There', *In Rainbows*

THE RAMONES

VOCAL/INSTRUMENTAL GROUP

The Ramones formed in 1974 in Forest Hills, New York, as Joey Ramone (born Jeffrey Hyman, vocals), Johnny Ramone (born John Cummings, guitar), Dee Dee Ramone (born Douglas Colvin, bass) and Tommy Ramone (born Tom Erdelyi, drums). They quickly gained a reputation with their 20-minute sets of two-minute songs, each counted in with a rapid 'one-two-three-four'. *Ramones* (1976), a low-budget album, created a stir in the emerging punk scene but did not make the American Top 100. DJ John Peel and a host of punk musicians-to-be were impressed, however, when The Ramones toured Britain soon after release.

Tommy left in 1978, worn out from touring, but stayed on to produce *Road To Ruin* (1978) that featured new drummer Marky (born Marc Bell) and songs that edged towards the three-minute mark, including the UK Top 40 'Don't Come Close'. In 1979, after the release of double live album *It's Alive* (1979), The Ramones starred in *Rock'n'Roll High School*, directed by B-movie maestro Roger Corman. Personnel changes diluted the band's appeal but they were still selling out shows right up to their last performance in Los Angeles in 1996. The band's irreverent attitude and three-minute songs will forever see them acclaimed as Godfathers of Punk.

GENRES

Punk Rock

ACTIVE YEARS

1974–96

CLASSIC RECORDINGS

Ramones, Leave Home, Rocket To Russia, 'Sheena Is A Punk Rocker', *Road To Ruin, End Of The Century*

RED HOT CHILI PEPPERS
VOCAL/INSTRUMENTAL GROUP

The Red Hot Chili Peppers met at Fairfax High School in Hollywood around 1980 and were influenced by funk, rap, jazz and punk rock. Anthony Kiedis (vocals) and Michael 'Flea' Balzary (bass) had recorded three albums when original guitarist Hillel Slovak died of a heroin overdose in 1988. They regrouped with teenager John Frusciante on guitar and Chad Smith on drums. The breakthrough came with 1991's Rick Rubin–produced *BloodSugarSexMagik* which went multi–platinum thanks to the untypical ballad 'Under The Bridge' – a hit single that made them international arena headliners. Other tracks like 'Funky Monks' and 'Suck My Kiss' rode on Flea's funky bass, their instrumental trademark.

Frusciante left the following year, former Jane's Addiction guitarist Dave Navarro filling in until Frusciante rejoined for 1999's *Californication*. This also saw Rick Rubin's return and was their most mature statement spawning four hit singles. The Peppers were now one of the biggest international live draws, a position confirmed with *By The Way* (2002), their first UK chart–topping album. Kiedis published his autobiography *Scar Tissue* in 2005 and 2006 saw the two–CD whammy of *Stadium Arcadium*. Josh Klinghoffer replaced the again absent Frusciante in 2009.

GENRES

Alternative Rock, Funk Rock, Rap Rock

ACTIVE YEARS

1983–present

CLASSIC RECORDINGS

'Knock Me Down', *BloodSugarSexMagic*, 'Under The Bridge', *One Hot Minute*, *Californication*, 'Scar Tissue', *By The Way*, *Stadium Arcadium*, 'Dani California'

R.E.M.

VOCAL/INSTRUMENTAL GROUP

Vocalist Michael Stipe met Peter Buck (guitar) in the Wuxtry record store in Athens, Georgia, in 1978. Two years later they met Bill Berry (drums) and Mike Mills (bass) at a party and Rapid Eye Movement – R.E.M. – was formed. By *Document* (1987) – their fifth album – R.E.M. were the biggest and most imitated band on the American alternative college circuit. Signing to Warners in 1987, their albums *Green* (1988) and *Out Of Time* (1991) catapulted them into the mainstream. As well as topping the US and UK album charts, addictive singles like 'Losing My Religion' and 'Shiny Happy People' became anthems at the height of the Nirvana–led grunge boom.

Automatic For The People (1992) was another classic yielding an astonishing five hit singles, including 'The Sidewinder Sleeps Tonight', 'Nightswimming', 'Everybody Hurts' and a tribute to comedian Andy Kaufman, 'Man On The Moon'. *Monster* (1994), however, returned to the guitar–heavy early days and since then their progress has been unpredictable as they follow their own course rather than courting popularity. The band (who have been without Bill Berry since 1997) were deservedly inducted into the Rock And Roll Hall Of Fame in 2007. The following year's *Accelerate*, their eighth UK chart–topper, was heralded as a return to form.

GENRES

Alternative Rock

ACTIVE YEARS

1980–present

CLASSIC RECORDINGS

Green, *Out Of Time*, 'Losing My Religion', 'Shiny Happy People', *Automatic For The People*, 'Everybody Hurts', *Monster*, *New Adventures In Hi-Fi*, *Accelerate*

SMOKEY ROBINSON & THE MIRACLES

VOCAL GROUP

The Miracles – Smokey Robinson, Claudette Rogers, Bobby Rogers, Ronnie White and Warren Moore – were a cornerstone of Motown's early success. Their 1960 hit 'Shop Around' set the gospel-and-soul tone for the label (later tempered with girl-group pop) and was influential across the pop board. The Beatles were fans and recorded 'You've Really Got A Hold On Me' in 1963, while Bob Dylan called Robinson 'America's greatest living poet'. Much later, in 1987, ABC recorded the original tribute 'When Smokey Sings'.

Robinson was also a producer and songwriter for other Motown acts, notably Mary Wells, The Temptations and The Marvelettes. 'I Second That Emotion' (1967) broke The Miracles in Britain, but Robinson had already decided to leave before 1970's reissued 'Tears Of A Clown' reached No. 1. Recording thereafter took second place to his vice-presidency of the label, a post he held from 1961 until Motown's sale to MCA in 1988. The 1975 album *Quiet Storm* lent its name to a new adult-orientated soul genre, in which he topped the charts with 1981's 'Being With You'. Robinson endured a torrid decade thereafter, with drugs and divorce, but pulled through. The Miracles had one more No. 1 without Robinson – 1976's 'Love Machine' – before splitting in 1978.

GENRES

Soul, R&B

ACTIVE YEARS

1955–72

CLASSIC RECORDINGS

'Shop Around', 'You've Really Got A Hold On Me', 'The Tracks Of My Tears', 'I Second That Emotion', 'Baby, Baby Don't Cry', 'The Tears Of A Clown'

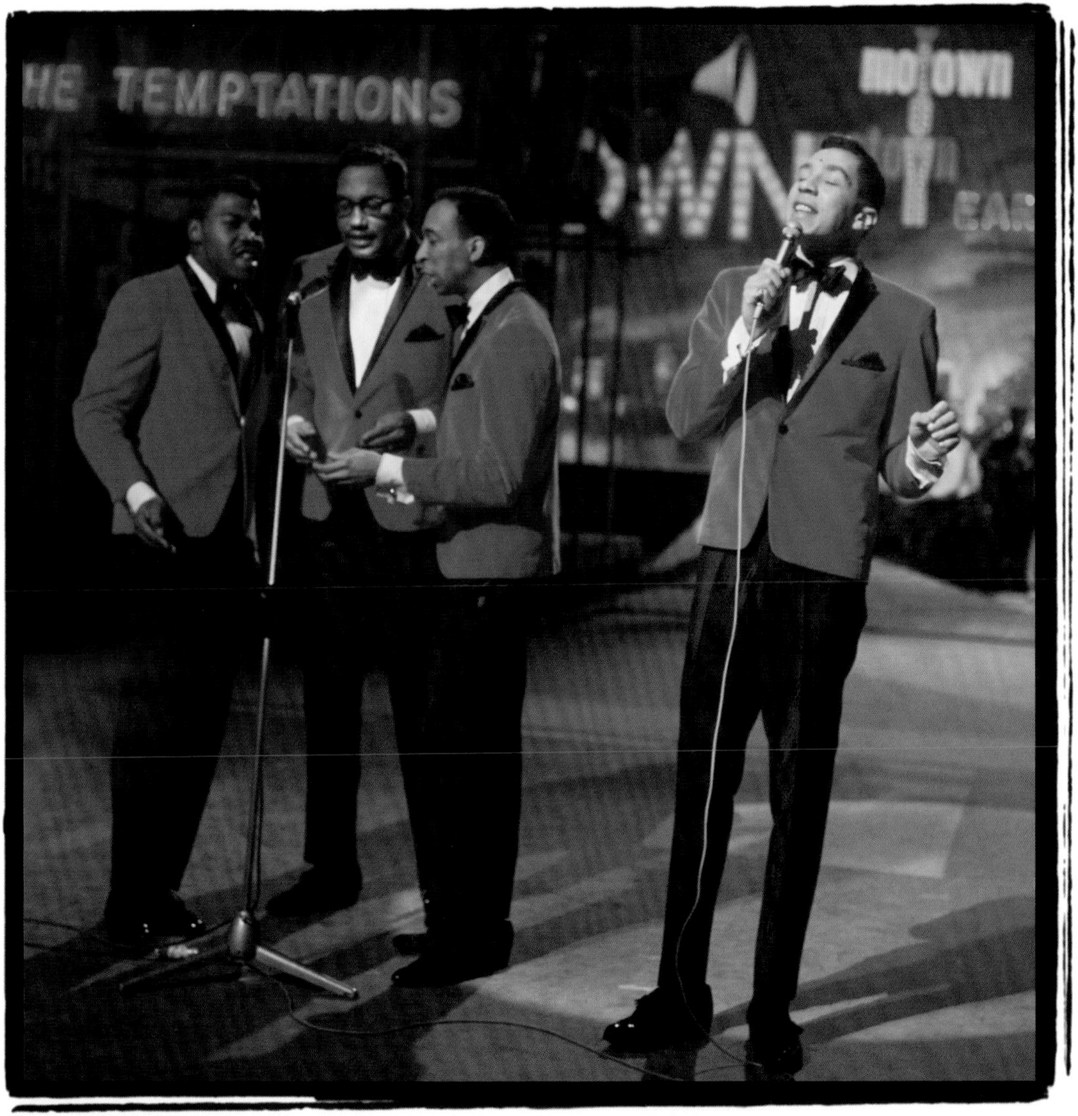
HE TEMPTATIONS

THE ROLLING STONES
VOCAL/INSTRUMENTAL GROUP

The Rolling Stones classic line-up featured singer/songwriter Mick Jagger, guitarist/songwriter Keith Richards, guitarist/multi-instrumentalist Brian Jones, bass player Bill Wyman (born William Perks) and drummer Charlie Watts. What came to be acclaimed and self-proclaimed as 'The World's Greatest Rock'n'Roll Band' first achieved success and notoriety as a loutish, parentally disapproved, blues-rock counterpoint to the equally contrived happy-go-lucky image of The Beatles.

Having first met as South London schoolboys, Jagger and Richards were reintroduced at the start of the 1960s by Dick Taylor, with whom Jagger played in a blues outfit named Little Boy Blue & The Blue Boys. Richards subsequently joined the band, and he and Jagger also made guest appearances for Alexis Korner's Blues Inc, befriending its drummer Charlie Watts as well as erstwhile member Brian Jones. Jones was trying to form a band of his own when he met Jagger and Richards. He had already recruited keyboard player Ian Stewart, and within a short time Mick and Keith joined the fold, along with Dick Taylor on bass and Mick Avory on drums.

The band made their debut at London's Marquee Club on 12 July 1962. Taylor was soon replaced by Bill Wyman. When Mick Avory also left the band, his place was taken by Tony Chapman, but he did not work out and in January 1963 The Stones recruited Charlie Watts.

BAD-BOY IMAGE

In April 1963, The Stones were checked out by a sharp young wheeler-dealer named Andrew Loog Oldham and signed to a management contract. Previously a publicist for Beatles' manager Brian Epstein, Oldham knew little about music but everything about promotion, and after The Stones secured a record contract with Decca, Oldham immediately forced conservative-looking Ian Stewart out of the official line-up.

TOP 100
ROCK ARTISTS

While The Rolling Stones released their first two R&B-flavoured singles, a cover of Chuck Berry's 'Come On' and the Lennon/McCartney-donated 'I Wanna Be Your Man', Oldham flirted with moulding them in The Beatles' lovable, smiling, clean-cut image. Then he thought better of it and, in a masterstroke, cast them as the anti-Fabs. 'Would you let your daughter marry a Rolling Stone?' was the main thrust of Oldham's ingenious press campaign, and his charges ran with it. Offstage, from many parents' point of view, things only got worse, as The Stones seemingly challenged the Establishment by flaunting their bad-boy image, culminating in several notorious and widely reported incidents.

Meanwhile, in the recording studio The Stones went from strength to strength. After 1964 saw the band enjoy UK chart-topping success with covers of 'It's All Over Now' and 'Little Red Rooster', they kicked off 1965 with the self-penned No. 1 'The Last Time' and followed this up with the worldwide smash that would become their anthem, '(I Can't Get No) Satisfaction', as well as the chart-topping 'Get Off Of My Cloud'.

EXPERIMENTATION AND TRAGEDY

Experimentation reared its head in 1966 with a variety of instruments being used on the ground-breaking *Aftermath*. The even more experimental *Between The Buttons* album followed in 1967, along with the controversially suggestive 'Let's Spend The Night Together' single. The release of *Their Satanic Majesties Request* (1967) album in December confirmed for many that flower power just did not suit The Stones.

Loog Oldham was soon replaced by Allen Klein and The Stones returned to form with the superb 'Jumpin' Jack Flash' single and musically eclectic *Beggar's Banquet* LP (both 1968). Behind the scenes, however, all was not well. Brian Jones resented Jagger and Richards' increasing domination of the band, and his chronic drug addiction prevented him from contributing in the studio. On 9 June 1969, Jones officially quit the band. Mick Taylor was drafted in to replace him, but just over three weeks later Brian Jones was found drowned in his swimming pool.

The *Let It Bleed* album and 'Honky Tonk Women' single (both 1969) maintained the run of chart success, yet tragedy continued to dog the band when a free concert staged at the Altamont Speedway resulted in the death of

a young black fan, Meredith Hunter, at the hands of Hell's Angels 'security guards'. For the next few years Jagger immersed himself more and more in the jet-set lifestyle and Richards retreated into his own drug-induced nightmare. Increased tensions between the two often adversely affected the quality their music.

REDEFINING THE STANDARDS

Still, there were flashes of the old genius with singles like 'Brown Sugar' and 'Angie', as well as the double-album *Exile On Main St.* (1972), which many would eventually hail as the band's masterpiece despite its initial critical drubbing. That same year, The Stones undertook a US tour that organizer Pete Rudge described as 'more like the Normandy landing', and thereafter the band would continue to lead the way and continually redefine the standards for lavish, large-scale stadium tours.

Mick Taylor left the group and was replaced by Ron Wood in 1974. Bill Wyman then departed in 1991. Yet, despite Mick Jagger's 1975 assertion that he would 'rather be dead than singing 'Satisfaction' when I'm forty-five,' he continues to break that pledge and, as shown by mid-period and later albums like *Some Girls* (1978), *Tattoo You* (1981), *Steel Wheels* (1989), *Voodoo Lounge* (1994) and most specifically *A Bigger Bang* (2005), he and his colleagues can still turn out worthy material and rock with the best of them.

GENRES

Rock, Rock'n'Roll, Blues Rock, R&B, Blues

ACTIVE YEARS

1962–present

CLASSIC RECORDINGS

'(I Can't Get No) Satisfaction', *Aftermath, Beggar's Banquet, Let It Bleed, Sticky Fingers, Exile On Main St., Some Girls, Tattoo You, A Bigger Bang*

ROXY MUSIC

VOCAL/INSTRUMENTAL GROUP

An enduringly influential British art rock group whose combination of futuristic music and 1950s rock'n'roll emerged in 1972 with their eponymous first album and standalone single 'Virginia Plain'. Fronted by singer Bryan Ferry, the Roxy Music line–up included synthesizer player/tape operator Brian Eno, Phil Manzanera (guitar), Andy McKay (saxophone), Paul Thompson (drums) and various bassists. When Eno left after *For Your Pleasure* (1973), Roxy's music lost some of its experimental edge but continued to plough a distinctive furrow through *Stranded* (1974) and *Country Life* (1975). Eno was replaced by classically trained keyboardist Eddie Jobson.

After *Siren* (1976), which contained their only US hit 'Love Is The Drug', Roxy Music took a break, reconvening two years later for *Manifesto* (1979). This along with *Flesh + Blood* (1980) and *Avalon* (1983) saw the band's music take on a glossy, commercial sheen. Roxy Music disbanded in 1983 and reformed sporadically from 1998 onwards, seemingly at the whim of Ferry whose solo career had always continued in parallel with the band's. Attempts to record new music were doomed to remain 'in the can,' and in 2009 Ferry insisted their future work together would be on a live basis only, though he collaborated with Eno in the studio.

GENRES

Art Rock, Glam Rock, New Wave

ACTIVE YEARS

1971–76, 1978–83, 1998–present

CLASSIC RECORDINGS

Roxy Music, 'Virginia Plain', *For Your Pleasure*, *Stranded*, *Country Life*, *Siren*, 'Love Is The Drug', *Flesh + Blood*, 'Jealous Guy', *Avalon*

TOP 100
ROCK ARTISTS

SANTANA

VOCAL/INSTRUMENTAL GROUP

A Latin-American take on what became known as jazz rock, the group led by Mexican Carlos Santana (guitar) was a major hit at Woodstock in 1969. 'Soul Sacrifice', the show-stopping climax to his act, was a highlight of the movie that followed, showing that the outfit formed as the Santana Blues Band three years earlier with bassist David Brown and keyboard-player/singer Gregg Rolie had finally arrived. This breakthrough coincided with an eponymous debut album penetrating the US Top 10 and the band's optimum commercial period, which included US chart-toppers *Abraxas* (1970) and *Santana III* (1971), plus hit singles like 'Evil Ways', 'Oye Como Va' and 'Black Magic Woman'. Carlos's smooth, legato playing style was the icing on a polyrhythmic cake, and while vocals were often an optional extra, the Santana sound was both distinctive and influential. Nicaraguan percussionist Jose 'Chepito' Areas was a key contributor.

A COMPLEX MIX

Santana himself became fascinated by Eastern religion, which led to an increased spirituality to the music. His love of jazz legends like John Coltrane and Miles Davis also brought complexity. This change of approach did not bode well in commercial terms, and also displeased some of his supporting musicians. Differences over drug use also surfaced and after 1972's jazzy *Caravanserai*, Carlos pursued outside album projects with, separately, John McLaughlin and Buddy Miles.

Group members came and went – drummer Michael Shrieve left after three albums and formed Automatic Man, while second guitarist Neal Schon, a teenager whose muscular playing had featured on *Santana III*, regrouped with founder member Gregg Rolie in 1974 to form the multi-platinum AOR outfit Journey. Their fame dwarfed the parent band, which endured a period of dwindling success, the 1977 hit 'She's Not There' providing one brief spark. Meanwhile, Carlos was a follower of guru Sri Chinmoy and was now known as Devadip – 'The lamp, light and eye of God'. (He later renounced Chinmoy in 1982.)

An appearance at Live Aid in 1985, after much string-pulling by one-time manager Bill Graham, showed Santana were still a dynamite live act, but record sales remained low and Santana left Columbia Records in 1990 after 22 years. Carlos was inducted into the Rock And Roll Hall Of Fame in 1998, but it seemed an epitaph on a career whose influence had been acknowledged by artists as diverse as Prince and Metallica's Kirk Hammett.

BACK ON TOP

Santana's rebirth was masterminded by his former Columbia Records boss Clive Davis and involved using guest vocalists like Matchbox 20's Rob Thomas, Michelle Branch and Wyclef Jean. The result was 1999's guest star-studded *Supernatural*, which spent 12 weeks at No. 1 in the US. It generated an all-time record-breaking nine Grammys in 2000, sparking off an on-going reversal of fortune. It paralleled John Lee Hooker, whose comeback album *The Healer* (1989) Carlos had guested on in tribute to an early influence.

'Smooth', his first US Top 40 hit since 1982 and his first chart-topping single ever, was followed to the summit by 'Maria Maria', while 2002's follow-up album *Shaman*, boasted another dazzling array of collaborators. *Rolling Stone* named Santana No. 15 on their list of the 100 Greatest Guitarists of All Time in 2003, while his cross-generational appeal was confirmed when he was featured in the computer music video game Guitar Hero 5. Latin music is now a very marketable commodity in the multi-cultural United States and beyond. Carlos Santana can claim, with justification, that he was in the forefront of the movement.

GENRES

Latin Rock, Jazz Rock, Funk, Hip Hop, Pop

ACTIVE YEARS

1966–present

CLASSIC RECORDINGS

Santana, *Abraxas*, 'Black Magic Woman', *Santana III*, *Caravanserai*, *Amigos*, *Supernatural*, 'Smooth', 'Maria Maria'

THE SEX PISTOLS

VOCAL/INSTRUMENTAL GROUP

Although they existed for just over two years, The Sex Pistols had more impact on the British music scene than any band since the 1960s. To the public they represented the face of punk. The Sex Pistols came together in London in 1975 under the aegis of boutique owner Malcolm McLaren. He turned his attention to a band featuring one of his shop assistants, bassist Glen Matlock, guitarist Steve Jones and drummer Paul Cook. With the inclusion of singer John 'Johnny Rotten' Lydon, The Sex Pistols signed to EMI and released a single, 'Anarchy In The UK', in 1976. The group's notoriety was assured when they swore on an early evening TV show. Matlock, who wrote most of the songs, was fired in March 1977 and replaced by Sid Vicious. 'God Save The Queen', coinciding with the Silver Jubilee celebrations in 1977, was banned by the BBC but reached No. 2 in the chart amid a widespread belief that it had been kept from the top.

Vicious died of a heroin overdose in 1979. The surviving Pistols reunited for the 'Filthy Lucre' world tour in 1996 and released *Filthy Lucre Live*. They played more shows sporadically thereafter, but spurned their Rock And Roll Hall Of Fame induction in 2006.

GENRES

Punk Rock

ACTIVE YEARS

1975–78

CLASSIC RECORDINGS

'Anarchy In The UK', *Never Mind The Bollocks*, 'God Save The Queen', 'Pretty Vacant', 'Holidays In The Sun', 'No One Is Innocent'

SIMON & GARFUNKEL

VOCAL DUO

As Tom & Jerry, Paul Simon (vocals, guitar) and Art Garfunkel (vocals) had a minor success as teenagers with 'Hey Schoolgirl' in 1957. Simon later went to the UK where he became a reliable draw in the country's folk clubs, but back in the US by 1964, he recorded an album, *Wednesday Morning 3am* with Garfunkel. Its highlight was 'The Sound Of Silence', which was issued (with superimposed backing) as a single that topped the US charts. With Simon taking most of the creative initiative, later hits included 'Homeward Bound' (1966), 'Mrs Robinson' (from 1968's *The Graduate* film soundtrack) and 'The Boxer' (1969). The new decade began with a No. 1 in both Britain and the States with 'Bridge Over Troubled Water' (1970) in which Garfunkel's breathy tenor floated effortlessly over orchestrated accompaniment. Occasional reunions on disc and on stage have proved lucrative, most notably for 1981's Concert in Central Park, in New York and a Rome show in 2004 that attracted 600,000.

Simon's solo career was the more significant, including 1986's *Graceland*, recorded with South African musicians and which put the country on the musical map. He owns his own solo catalogue and has a singer–songwriter son, Harper. Garfunkel scored UK chart-toppers with 'I Only Have Eyes For You' (1975) and 'Bright Eyes' (1979).

GENRES

Folk Rock, Soft Rock

ACTIVE YEARS

1957–70

CLASSIC RECORDINGS

'Hey Schoolgirl', 'The Sounds Of Silence', 'Mrs Robinson', *Bridge Over Troubled Water*, 'The Boxer', 'Bridge Over Troubled Water', 'Cecilia'

TOP 100
ROCK ARTISTS

SLY & THE FAMILY STONE

VOCAL/INSTRUMENTAL GROUP

The story of Sly Stone (born Sylvester Stewart) is a classic rock'n'roll tale of ground-breaking success followed by a drug-fuelled downward spiral into unreliability and dissipation. In 1967, Stewart formed Sly & The Family Stone whose members came from several racial backgrounds. Their second LP, 1968's *Dance To The Music*, saw the band hit its stride. The result of free-flowing hippy spirit applied to soul music was an exuberant riot of vocal and instrumental interplay. An early 1969 single 'Everyday People' became the group's first US No. 1 with its engaging chant 'Different strokes for different folks'. Their fourth LP, *Stand!* (1969), spent over 100 weeks in the charts, while The Family Stone's career-defining performance at Woodstock that year stole the show.

Sly was meanwhile developing a serious cocaine habit and becoming unpredictable. The much delayed *There's A Riot Goin' On* (1971) was an expression of the fractured society of the early 1970s after the optimism of the late 1960s. Both the album and the first single from it – 'Family Affair' – were US No. 1s. Sly focused temporarily for 1973's *Fresh*, but it was his last great album. On his induction into the Rock And Roll Hall Of Fame in 1993 he was reportedly living in sheltered housing, and today he remains largely overlooked.

GENRES

Funk, Soul, Rock, Psychedelic

ACTIVE YEARS

1967–75

CLASSIC RECORDINGS

'Dance To The Music', *Stand!*, 'Everyday People', 'Thank You (Falettinme Be Mice Elf Agin)', *There's A Riot Goin' On*, 'Family Affair', *Fresh*

BRUCE SPRINGSTEEN & THE E STREET BAND

VOCAL/INSTRUMENTAL GROUP

Hailed as the new Dylan, New Jersey's Bruce Springsteen was signed to Columbia/CBS by John Hammond, the man who spotted Dylan's potential a decade earlier. While Springsteen's first two albums, *Greetings From Asbury Park, N.J.* and *The Wild, The Innocent & The E Street Shuffle* (both 1973), mined youthful experience on the boardwalks and amusement arcades of his hometown, it was his incendiary live performances with The E Street Band that caused *Rolling Stone* critic (and his future manager) Jon Landau to exclaim in print: 'I saw the future of rock'n'roll, and its name is Bruce Springsteen.' The twin keyboards of Danny Federici and David Sancious (later replaced by Roy Bittan) were backed by the thunderous rhythm section of Garry Tallent and Max Weinberg. Guitarist Steve Van Zandt was his long-standing right-hand man, the pair having played together in New Jersey clubs.

THE NEXT BIG THING

Springsteen fully realized his potential with the widescreen *Born To Run* (1975). In an unprecedented coincidence, US current affairs magazines *Time* and *Newsweek* – neither of which was particularly 'rock-friendly' – both independently featured fast-rising Bruce Springsteen on their covers. The singer and his group The E Street Band took America by storm with the album and its titular single, the former reaching the Top 3 after entering the chart the previous month.

The songs and performances that brought Springsteen overnight success were built on classic foundations, mixing Roy Orbison's emotive vocal delivery and Dylan's lyrical complexity with a kitchen-sink production reminiscent of Phil Spector's multi-layered 'Wall of Sound'. He was aided by larger-than-life saxophonist Clarence Clemons who features on the album cover with 'The Boss' in a pose that has since become an enduring rock image.

Posters featuring Landau's hyperbolic quote were torn down by Springsteen himself, who was clearly feeling the pressure of being the 'next big thing'. So much so that, after a bomb scare emptied the Uptown Theatre in Milwaukee, the normally sober Springsteen returned to the venue from his hotel on the roof of his car, having apparently downed a few calming slugs of liquor.

NEW DIMENSIONS

Managerial problems delayed *Darkness On The Edge Of Town* (1978), a more sombre but no less compelling work than *Born To Run*. In the interim Springsteen stayed on the road to hone his stagecraft, premiere new songs and build a fanbase that would support him throughout his career. The double album *The River* appeared in 1980 and was an indication that his stockpile of songs remained as high as ever. This album was followed by the stark, pessimistic *Nebraska* in 1982. A solo effort recorded in a hotel room on a portable studio, it evoked comparisons with Johnny Cash, Pete Seeger, Woody Guthrie and other acoustic-roots chronicles of depression-struck America.

Taking yet another turn and reunited with The E Street Band, Springsteen made his pitch to enter the worldwide showbiz mainstream with 1984's *Born In The USA*. It went quadruple platinum in the UK and sold 14 million copies across the globe. His world tour was seen by an estimated two million people. By this time, Nils Lofgren had taken over from Van Zandt who was enjoying a solo career, but when that faded he was welcomed back into the ranks. *Born In The USA*'s title track was controversially used for President Ronald Regan's 1984 re-election campaign, its double-edged message notwithstanding. 'Dancing In The Dark' gave Springsteen his first UK Top 10 single when re-released in 1985. The video featured a young Courtney Cox, later of *Friends* fame.

THE ULTIMATE PERFORMER

Springsteen maintained a sense of intimacy during stadium shows by talking to the audience. Another feature of his gigs was their length, often in excess of four hours. Backed by The E Street Band, Springsteen was without equal as a live performer, as documented on the 1986 five-record epic *Live/1975–85*.

Springsteen opted for a more intimate approach for *Tunnel Of Love* (1987), his last work with The E Street Band for over a decade. Though a difficult time for Springsteen personally, as he was going through a divorce with actress first wife Julianne Phillips, the period was most successful professionally, as *Tunnel...* was his sixth consecutive Top 5 LP.

BACK TO HIS ROOTS

In 1995 Springsteen surprised his public after a couple of relatively anodyne albums by going back to folk roots. *The Ghost Of Tom Joad* was a solo effort similar to *Nebraska* that may yet be reassessed as its predecessor was. The previous year had seen him win an Academy Award for his one-off song 'Streets Of Philadelphia', which appeared on the soundtrack to the 1993 film *Philadelphia*. In 1999, Springsteen & The E Street Band officially got together again and went on an extensive Reunion Tour, the New York dates of which were released as a CD and DVD. Their first album together, *The Rising*, was released in 2002 and reflected the recent 9/11 attacks. Band-backed albums like *Magic* (2007) and *Working On A Dream* (2009) have been interspersed with solo efforts like 2005's *Dreams & Dust* and 2006's *We Shall Overcome: The Seeger Sessions*. The latter involved other musicians, but only backing singer/wife Patti Scialfa from his band.

Still rocking on into his sixties, Springsteen continues to show everyone who's 'The Boss'. He's never betrayed his working-class roots, and has inspired the likes of John Mellencamp to follow in his footsteps. The only thing he hasn't done – yet – is outlast Bob Dylan.

GENRES

Rock, Folk Rock, Pop

ACTIVE YEARS

1972–present

CLASSIC RECORDINGS

Born To Run, Darkness On The Edge Of Town, The River, Nebraska, Born In The USA, Live/1975–85, Tunnel Of Love, 'Streets Of Philadelphia', The Rising

STATUS QUO
VOCAL/INSTRUMENTAL GROUP

The great survivors of British rock, Status Quo are synonymous with three–chord boogie. They first came to public attention in 1967 with the psychedelically flavoured single 'Picture Of Matchstick Men' (their only US Top 20 hit). A change of direction to their more familiar style was heralded by the single 'Down The Dustpipe' and explored more fully on the 1970 album *Ma Kelly's Greasy Spoon*. The line-up coalesced around the ever–present duo of Francis Rossi (guitar, vocals) and Rick Parfitt (guitar) with Alan Lancaster (bass) and Richard Coughlan (drums).

Bedecked in denim and plimsolls, Quo were a potent live force, consolidating their popularity with a string of consistent albums *Piledriver*, *Hello* (both 1973), *Quo* (1974), *On The Level* (1975) and *Blue For You* (1976). Their many hits include 1973's 'Caroline' (their only UK singles chart topper), 'Down Down' (1974) and the song that would open Live Aid, John Fogerty's 'Rocking All Over The World' (1975). Estrangement from Alan Lancaster, who emigrated to Australia, followed by Coughlan's departure, led to Quo thenceforth being perceived and marketed as Rossi and Parfitt. It should be said that keyboardist Andy Bown and bassist John 'Rhino' Edwards have now served longer than those originals. 'The Quo' continue in the current century, despite Rossi cutting off his ponytail for charity and trying a solo career.

GENRES

Boogie Rock, Psychedelic Rock, Hard Rock

ACTIVE YEARS

1967–present

CLASSIC RECORDINGS

'Pictures Of Matchstick Men', *Hello!*, 'Caroline', *Quo*, *On The Level*, 'Down Down', *Blue For You*, 'Rockin' All Over The World'

ROD STEWART

VOCALS

One of the UK's finest vocalists, Roderick David Stewart was born in London to Scottish parents. After singing with The Hoochie Coochie Men in 1964 alongside Long John Baldry, Stewart joined The Jeff Beck Group in 1967 alongside bassist Ron Wood. There he developed his rasping vocal style on two seminal albums: *Truth* (1968) and *Beck-Ola* (1969). He also signed a solo deal.

When Beck disbanded his group in 1969, Stewart and Wood formed The Faces with former Small Faces Ian McLagan, Ronnie Lane and Kenney Jones. He still maintained his solo career and *Every Picture Tells A Story* and single, 'Maggie May' (both 1971) held the UK No. 1 single and album in the UK and US for a week. Two months later The Faces' *A Nod's As Good As A Wink To A Blind Horse* (1971) got to No. 2 in the UK and No. 6 in the US. From then on the relationship between Stewart and The Faces was uneasy. Stewart moved to Los Angeles and released *Atlantic Crossing* (1975), recorded at Muscle Shoals with most of Booker T & The MGs and veteran producer Tom Dowd. He has never surpassed this in the rock field, though a series of *Great American Songbook* albums beginning in 2002 have revitalized his career since beating thyroid cancer.

GENRES

Rock, Pop, Disco

ACTIVE YEARS

1964–present

CLASSIC RECORDINGS

'Maggie May', *Atlantic Crossing, A Night On The Town, Foot Loose & Fancy Free, Blondes Have More Fun*, 'Da Ya Think I'm Sexy?'

T. REX

VOCAL/INSTRUMENTAL GROUP

The first glam rock band evolved from acoustic duo Tyrannosaurus Rex, formed by Marc Bolan (guitar, vocals) and multi-instrumentalist Steve Peregrine-Took. Mickey Finn (bongos) replaced Took in 1969 as Bolan began to deploy electric instruments. Shortening the name to T. Rex heralded a chart breakthrough in October 1970 with the single 'Ride A White Swan'. Steve Currie (bass) and Bill Legend (drums) were added and T. Rex achieved a further 10 Top 10 singles, including four No. 1s, as Bolan became a teen idol. Much credit should have gone to producer Tony Visconti for tracks like 'Get It On', a US Top 10 hit in 1972 that (falsely) suggested a major US breakthrough. A movie with Ringo Starr, *Born To Boogie* (1972), also promised much but disappointed.

Back at home, by 1973 the formula of Chuck Berry riffs and unfathomable lyrics was starting to wear thin. Bolan's popularity slipped away until a new generation hailed him as one of punk's forefathers and he was granted his own TV show to play host to them. Bolan died in a car accident in September 1977, but his fame lives on thanks to tribute acts like Britain's T. Rextasy that re-create his stage act to the very last sequin.

GENRES

Glam Rock

ACTIVE YEARS

1967–77

CLASSIC RECORDINGS

'Ride A White Swan', 'Hot Love', *Electric Warrior*, 'Get It On', 'Telegram Sam', 'Metal Guru', 'Children Of The Revolution', '20th Century Boy'

TINA TURNER
VOCALS

An American soul/rock singer, Tina Turner was famous initially as part of a husband and wife duo with Ike. The pair enjoyed several hits in the 1960s and established a formidable reputation as a live act, largely due to Tina's stage presence. The couple's last major success was 1973's 'Nutbush City Limits', a UK Top 5 hit. Weary of Ike's mental and physical abuse, she left him mid–tour in 1976 and embarked on a solo career soon afterwards. However, it was not until *Private Dancer* (1984) that Tina found the formula that would make her one of the biggest names in 1980s music. Made with the assistance of famous friends like Mark Knopfler and Jeff Beck, the album sold over 20 million copies. The successful follow–ups *Break Every Rule* (1986) and *Foreign Affair* (1989) showed that her remarkable comeback was no flash in the pan.

On the death of Ike in 2007, she issued this statement: 'Tina hasn't had any contact with Ike in more than 30 years. No further comment will be made.' Yet the following year saw her emerge from semi–retirement in Switzerland to perform with Beyoncé at the Grammys. In 2008 she embarked on her Tina!: 50th Anniversary Tour, which became one of the highest–selling series of shows of 2008–09.

GENRES

Rock, Soul, Pop

ACTIVE YEARS

1958–present

CLASSIC RECORDINGS

Private Dancer, 'Let's Stay Together', 'What's Love Got To Do With It', 'We Don't Need Another Hero', *Break Every Rule*, *Foreign Affair*, 'The Best'

U2

VOCAL/INSTRUMENTAL GROUP

Singer Bono (born Paul Hewson), guitarist The Edge (born David Evans), bassist Adam Clayton and drummer Larry Mullen Jr formed a band at school in Dublin in 1976. Settling on the name U2 in 1978, they came to England in 1980. Three flop singles preceded their debut album *Boy* (1980), a well-received work concerning adolescence. Constant gigging, including a first visit to America, helped establish their formidable reputation as live performers. Minor hits 'Fire' and 'Gloria' were taken from the religiously themed *October* (1981), regarded as one of U2's least-satisfying albums.

U2's long-awaited chart breakthrough came with the typically passionate 'New Year's Day' from 1983's *War*. The live mini-album *Under A Blood Red Sky* (1984) was a largely successful attempt to capture U2's live act, its version of 'Sunday Bloody Sunday' eclipsing the original on *War*. The album earned them their first US Top 30 placing.

U2 continued to gather momentum with *The Unforgettable Fire* (1984), featuring 'Pride (In The Name Of Love)'. The band's anthemic music acquired a new depth via the atmospheric production by Daniel Lanois and Brian Eno. It cracked the Top 20 in America, fitting for an album that revealed U2's growing fascination with the United States.

A PIVOTAL PERFORMANCE

Live Aid proved a pivotal moment in the band's ascension into the major league. An unforgettable performance at Wembley Stadium preceded the eagerly anticipated *The Joshua Tree* (1987), which did not disappoint. Again produced by Lanois and Eno, a widescreen element was added to the band's stirring rock music. The first three tracks were all hit singles – 'Where The Streets Have No Name', 'I Still Haven't Found What I'm Looking For' and 'With Or Without You' – all encapsulating the album's themes of spirituality and soul-searching. *The Joshua Tree* went on to sell 25 million copies worldwide.

This was quickly followed by *Rattle And Hum* (1988), a part–live/part–studio double set that also served as the soundtrack to U2's documentary film of the same name, a memento of *The Joshua Tree* tour. It sold well and gave the band their first UK No. 1 single, 'Desire'.

AMBITIOUS ALBUMS

Achtung Baby (1991) was a deliberate attempt to forge a new direction, incorporating elements of dance and electronica. Even more ambitious was *Zooropa* (1993), recorded between legs of the extravagantly staged Zoo TV tour and influenced by its theme of media overkill. U2 began to reinvent themselves, producing an ambient–leaning album totally unlike their previous work. The ironically entitled *Pop* (1997) completed U2's transformation into a post–modern rock band on an album that featured familiar themes of love, desire and faith in crisis. It was one of the band's lesser-selling albums, although 'Discotheque' was a British No. 1 single. The accompanying Popmart tour was another visual extravaganza. The gap between new albums was filled by *The Best Of 1980–90* (1998). Next came the back–to–basics approach of *All That You Can't Leave Behind* (2000), which reunited the band with producers Lanois and Eno. The album yielded a UK chart topper in 'Beautiful Day'.

Parallel to his music, Bono has been increasingly involved in economic/humanitarian concerns. He returned to U2 to participate in *How To Dismantle An Atomic Bomb* (2004), spawning yet more UK No. 1s in 'Vertigo' and 'Sometimes You Can't Make It On Your Own'. *No Line On the Horizon* (2009) proved a disappointment, however.

GENRES

Rock, Alternative Rock, Pop

ACTIVE YEARS

1976–present

CLASSIC RECORDINGS

'Pride (In The Name Of Love)', *The Joshua Tree*, 'With Or Without You', *Rattle And Hum*, 'Desire', *Achtung Baby*, 'Beautiful Day', 'Vertigo'

312

TOP 100 ROCK ARTISTS

VAN HALEN
VOCAL/INSTRUMENTAL GROUP

As the 1970s advanced past its midpoint, Clapton, Beck and Page had either faded away or semi-retired. The band Van Halen stepped out of sun-soaked Pasadena, California, to define the US heavy metal scene for a decade. Every generation needs its guitar hero, and the stage was set for Dutch-born Eddie Van Halen. The band boasted a dashing, tuneful frontman in Dave Lee Roth (vocals), a wizard guitarist in Eddie Van Halen and rocking pop tunes, as 1978's debut album *Van Halen* proved. Eddie's brother Alex (drums) and Michael Anthony (bass) completed this golden gang. Eddie used a home-made axe nicknamed the 'Frankenstrat' with a distinctive black and red paint job.

A NEW GUITAR HERO

The eponymous debut album would never be equalled, ranking alongside *Led Zeppelin* (1969) and *Are You Experienced?* (1967) and establishing a new stadium-rock benchmark. Van Halen's father Jan was a saxophone player, and Eddie has since suggested he was trying to create a horn-like tone with his guitar. On the basis of that one album, lead singer David Lee Roth was moved to state: 'Eddie Van Halen is the first guitar hero of the 1980s; all the other guitar heroes are dead.' *Guitar World* writer Dan Amrich amplified the point some years later: 'Before 1978, guitar just had to be loud. After Van Halen arrived it had to be loud and *fast*.' *Van Halen II* (1979) consolidated their position, entering the US Top 10, and in 1983 Eddie provided the dazzling solo to Michael Jackson's 'Beat It'. But it was 1984's *1984* and its attendant pop metal smash 'Jump' that promoted the band to pop superstar status. Ironically, the instrumental hook on the US No. 1 single was played by Eddie on a keyboard rather than a guitar.

Roth left for a solo career and Sammy Hagar took over with no effect on chart placings – during the 1980s Van Halen had more *Billboard* Hot 100 hits than any other hard rock or heavy metal band – but a definite diminution in charisma.

TOP 100 ROCK ARTISTS

It's one of rock's ironies that their first US chart-topping album, *5150* (named after the police code for a criminally insane person) didn't happen until 1986, the year after Van Halen and Roth had gone their separate ways. Influential producer Ted Templeman went too, having pledged himself to the singer. Roth enjoyed a sporadically successful solo career in which he was abetted by hotshot young guitarist Steve Vai.

THE EVER-CHANGING LINE-UP

When Hagar also left in 1996, Roth returned to record two new songs before Extreme's Gary Cherone briefly filled the berth. In 2004 Eddie began to sell his own design of Charvel guitars called 'EVH Art Series Guitars' modelled on his earlier 'Frankenstrat' guitar right down to the volume pot being replaced with a tone knob just like the original. A reunion tour with Roth took place in 2007 after Eddie's successful battle with cancer. Eddie's son Wolfgang was brought in on bass, but some cynics sensed that commercial reasons weighed heavier than creativity.

Few guitarists who've operated in the hard-rock field in the last three decades can claim they've not been influenced, or at least inspired at some point, by Eddie Van Halen. In January 1998 *Guitarist* magazine listed its top 100 solos, and 'Eruption' from the mighty first Van Halen album stood proud at No. 2.

GENRES

Hard Rock, Heavy Metal

ACTIVE YEARS

1974–99, 2004, 2007–08

CLASSIC RECORDINGS

Van Halen, Van Halen II, Women And Children First, 1984, 'Jump', *5150*, 'Why Can't This Be Love', *OU812*, 'When It's Love'

THE VELVET UNDERGROUND

VOCAL/INSTRUMENTAL GROUP

The Velvet Underground were offbeat, daring, challenging, provocative, sometimes outrageous and always different. During the wildly experimental and progressive second half of the 1960s, they were the avant-rock outfit par excellence. Fronted by lead singer/songwriter/guitarist Lou Reed, their classic line-up included bass/viola player John Cale, Sterling Morrison on guitar and drummer Maureen Tucker. Andy Warhol protégée Nico (born Christa Paffgen) joined them on classic first album, *The Velvet Underground & Nico* (also known as 'The Banana Album' courtesy of Warhol's cover art). This record's brilliantly eclectic mix of songs – many culled from their aforementioned live set – failed to ignite sales or light up radio dials upon its release in January 1967, but it would have an indelible influence on subsequent generations of offbeat musos and performance artists.

Reed's departure in 1970 effectively ended the band, though they staggered on until 1973. Their influence quickly became apparent in the likes of Roxy Music, and their ground-breaking music subsequently cultivated a strong cult following while heavily influencing the punk/new-wave generation. Songs Like 'I'm Waiting For The Man' and 'Heroin' (both 1967) and 'White Light/White Heat' (1968) are rightly regarded as classics, while Reed's solo career continues to throw up the occasional gem.

GENRES

Experimental Rock, Art Rock

ACTIVE YEARS

1965–73, 1992–94

CLASSIC RECORDINGS

The Velvet Underground & Nico, *White Light/White Heat*, 'Sister Ray', *The Velvet Underground*, *Loaded*

TOP 100
ROCK ARTISTS

THE WHITE STRIPES
VOCAL/INSTRUMENTAL DUO

Divorcées Jack (vocals, guitar) and Meg White (percussion) formed The White Stripes with the mission statement of keeping a childlike simplicity in their music and imagery. Dressing only in red, white and black and playing a thrilling version of blues and rock (owing as much to Led Zeppelin as pioneers like Son House and Lead Belly), the pair found mass international acclaim with third album *White Blood Cells* (2001), which married Jack's jackhammer riffing with a more tender, acoustic side (most notably on single 'Hotel Yorba'). Their next album *Elephant* (2003, recorded in a fortnight on a shoestring budget, then receiving massive sales figures) explored multi-tracked vocals, and the follow-up *Get Behind Me Satan* (2005) saw an even darker approach employed, often incorporating marimbas and xylophones. By 2010, their acclaimed output consisted of six studio albums, two EPs, one concert film, 26 singles and 14 music videos.

White (real name John Anthony Gillis) has a seemingly insatiable appetite for recording and performing. He has run two groups in parallel with The White Stripes, The Raconteurs (formed in 2005) and The Dead Weather, established 2009, in which he plays drums. He's also collaborated with Dylan, Jeff Beck, Alicia Keys and others.

GENRES

Punk Blues, Alternative Rock, Pop Rock

ACTIVE YEARS

1997–present

CLASSIC RECORDINGS

White Blood Cells, 'Hotel Yorba', *Elephant*, 'Seven Nation Army', *Get Behind Me Satan*, 'Blue Orchid', *Icky Thump*, 'Icky Thump'

THE WHO

VOCAL/INSTRUMENTAL GROUP

The success of The Who was down to the combination of four very different individuals and the fabulous songs of guitarist Pete Townshend. Comprising Townshend on guitar, Roger Daltrey on vocals, John Entwistle on bass and Keith Moon on drums, The Who virtually exploded onto the mid–1960s scene in a blaze of power rock that placed them at the forefront of the mod movement.

The Who's stage act saw Townshend leap into the air, strike ear–shattering chords with a swirling windmill motion and smash his guitar, while Daltrey, swaggering menacingly, swung his microphone like a lasso. Moon went berserk on the drums and Entwistle stood without motion or expression. Reinforced by Townshend's songwriting, this London outfit helped define teen rebellion while continually pushing the sonic envelope.

After meeting in their native west London neighbourhood of Shepherds Bush during their early teens, Townshend and Entwistle joined a Dixieland band in which the former played banjo and the latter played trumpet. They then formed a rock'n'roll outfit, before Entwistle left in 1962 to join a band named The Detours that included Roger Daltrey in its line-up. Daltrey replaced Colin Dawson on lead vocals shortly after Townshend joined as a rhythm guitarist, and that same year, 1963, drummer Doug Sandom was replaced by Keith Moon.

THE MOD YEARS

In early 1964, The Detours became The Who, and while still semi–professional they secured regular bookings at London's Marquee club. It was there that Townshend, frustrated with the sound system, first smashed one of his guitars, and where the group caught the attention of manager Peter Meaden. With Meaden at the helm, The Who became The High Numbers, adopted a sharp mod image and released the Meaden-penned single 'I'm The Face'/'Zoot Suit'.

The record sank without a trace and took Meaden with it, to be replaced by Chris Stamp and Kit Lambert. The High Numbers reverted to The Who and built a sturdy following courtesy of their animated stage performances and solid R&B repertoire.

A contract with Decca Records placed the band with Kinks' producer Shel Talmy, a relationship that yielded the UK hit singles 'I Can't Explain', 'Anyway, Anyhow, Anywhere' and 'My Generation', featuring Daltrey alternately stuttering and belting out Townshend's lyrics, including the anthemic reckless-youth line, 'I hope I die before I get old'. Onstage this message was reinforced not only by Townshend's guitar-smashing antics, but also by Keith Moon regularly demolishing his kit. The string of UK Top 10 hits continued in 1966 with 'Substitute', although this marked the end of The Who's collaboration with Shel Talmy.

Kit Lambert now took over the production reins, and in 1967 the band at last achieved American success when *Happy Jack* (originally titled *A Quick One* in Britain) cracked the Top 40 and 'I Can See For Miles' made the Top 10, resulting in the band's dynamic appearance at the Monterey Pop Festival in June of that year. The Who had finally arrived, yet the mod movement was winding down, prompting Pete Townshend to regroup and compose what many consider to be his masterpiece, the rock opera *Tommy* (1969).

THE TRIUMPH OF TOMMY

Released to widespread acclaim and huge sales, the double album about a deaf, dumb and blind child was performed in its entirety during The Who's 1969 tour, which included prestigious dates at the London Coliseum and New York's Metropolitan Opera House. *Tommy* would later resurface as a play, a 1975 movie starring Daltrey, and a 1993 Broadway musical. As a logical progression to the serious critical attention lavished on The Beatles' masterpiece *Sgt Pepper* album, *Tommy* transformed rock into a neo-classical art form. Unafraid to use the LP record as a broad canvas, Townshend wrote two rock operas in *Tommy* and the later *Quadrophenia* (1973) that defined the genre. Whether casting singer Roger Daltrey in the role of the 'deaf dumb and blind' Tommy or painting the mod culture he'd grown up in, Townshend's evocative use of words and bold, slashing guitar chords was impressive.

The Who would not find it easy to live up to *Tommy*'s reputation, although the band still enjoyed considerable success with further hit singles and acclaimed albums such as *Who's Next* (1971), a fine album that was salvaged from the aborted sci-fi concept Lifehouse. The classic anti-politics anthem 'Won't Get Fooled Again', violin-led 'Baba O'Riley' and sinister 'Behind Blue Eyes' were all classics.

MUSICAL LEGACY

After *The Who By Numbers* (1975), *Who Are You* (1978) turned out to be just as average. Its title track was Townshend's self-searching response to punk – but ironically the new wave embraced his honesty, Paul Weller just one admitted acolyte. Townshend's songs came from his reactions to current events, but this has meant some songs like 'My Generation' have worn less well than others.

Who Are You was the band's last outing with Keith Moon. The drummer's famously debauched sex, drugs and rock'n'roll lifestyle caught up with him in 1978, at the age of just 31. Although there would be more recordings and numerous tours with others filling Moon's larger-than-life shoes, Townshend, Daltrey and Entwistle (who died in 2002) would subsequently concede that The Who really died along with its enigmatic, manically virtuosic drummer.

GENRES
Rock, Pop, Hard Rock

ACTIVE YEARS
1964–82, 1989, 1996–present

CLASSIC RECORDINGS
'Anyway, Anyhow, Anywhere', 'My Generation', 'I Can See For Miles', 'Magic Bus', *Tommy*, 'Pinball Wizard', *Who's Next*, *Quadrophenia*

STEVIE WONDER

PIANO, VOCALS

Born Steveland Judkins and blind from shortly after birth, the future Stevie Wonder was already singing in his local choir at the age of four. By the time he was seven he had mastered the piano, harmonica and drums. In 1961, Ronnie White of The Miracles introduced the child prodigy to the label's founder Berry Gordy, who signed him up as Little Stevie Wonder to a long-term contract. Early releases made much of his instrumental virtuosity (which now extended to organ and vocals) and of parallels with another blind soulful singer, Ray Charles. In 1963, his third single was his breakthrough. An edited version of the largely instrumental 'Fingertips' from live album *The 12-Year Old Genius* went to No. 1 in both the pop and the R&B charts in the US, the first live single to do so. The album followed in its wake, Motown's first chart-topping LP.

THE FREEDOM TO WRITE

The 1960s saw Stevie Wonder grow from child star to soul man. He dropped the 'Little' as early as 1964, and his vocal performances developed their trademark tone: pure, full, warm, the soulful embodiment of R&B. Wonder was one of the very first pop artists to embrace the emerging world of electronic keyboards. He was, however, becoming increasingly frustrated by the constraints of Motown's hit-making machine. In 1964, he had his first co-written hit, 'Uptight (Everything's Alright)', a US million-seller, which two years later would open his chart account in the UK. From now on he would write more and more of his output, and in 1968 he was able to claim co-writing credits for half of the album *For Once In My Life*.

The 1971 album *Where I'm Coming From* was a coherent set of compositions, increasingly dominated by Wonder's keyboard arrangements and entirely produced and co-written by him. It generated only one hit single, 'If You Really Love Me', but was a manifesto for the future. On his twenty-first birthday, Wonder negotiated a deal that

gave him complete control of his output. *Music Of My Mind*, the first fruit of the new deal released in 1972, saw Wonder play all but one of the instruments. The writing and arrangements showed a new depth, and his ability to breathe life and warmth into synthesizers would become his defining sound.

ALWAYS AN ACTIVIST

Supporting The Rolling Stones on their US tour exposed him to a massive new rock audience. His next two singles went to No. 1 in the US (Nos. 11 and 7 in the UK), the funk-soul groove and social concerns of 'Superstition' contrasting with the deceptively simple ballad 'You Are The Sunshine Of My Life'. The 1973 album from which they were drawn, *Talking Book*, was his most well-rounded and personal to date. It was followed by late 1973's outward-looking *Innervisions*, a powerful and comprehensive discussion of America's social confusion, with hit singles 'Higher Ground', 'Living For The City' and 'He's Misstra Know It All'. After surviving a near fatal car crash, 1974's *Fulfillingness' First Finale* was more introspective but found time for the No. 1 political barb 'You Haven't Done Nothin''.

The three albums of 1973–74 earned him a total of nine Grammy Awards, enabling Wonder to negotiate the richest ever recording deal in 1975: $13 million over seven years. A year later he delivered his masterpiece, *Songs In The Key Of Life*, a double LP plus bonus EP that produced a glorious run of hits including two more US No. 1s – the party funk 'I Wish' and a big band jazz tribute to 'Sir Duke' Ellington. Other highlights were 'Another Star' with its swirling Latin rhythms and the beautiful mid-tempo soul ballad 'Isn't She Lovely' (a celebration of the birth of his daughter Aisha). It spent a total of 14 weeks at No. 1 in the US and won the singer another five Grammy Awards.

In the years that followed, Stevie Wonder struggled to emulate that artistic and commercial pinnacle. Discounting a largely instrumental soundtrack album, the first real follow-up, *Hotter Than July* (a 1980 single LP), seemed a little insubstantial after a four-year gap. It still yielded four hits including 'Masterblaster', his tribute to Bob Marley, and the album's closing track 'Happy Birthday', his anthem to Martin Luther King Jr that helped the civil rights icon's birthday be recognized as a national holiday in the US.

The early 1980s saw Wonder release only a handful of singles. After another five-year gap, the 1985 set *In Square Circle* showed Wonder comfortably adopting new technologies of keyboard programming. But he had lost momentum. This and its follow-up in 1987, *Characters*, kept him in the chart but he now seemed content to tread water.

A SOUL STATESMAN

Wonder settled into the role of elder soul statesman, and much of the 1980s was filled by a round of celebrity tribute performances and lifetime-achievement award ceremonies. After another long break, 1995's *Conversation Peace* was a disappointingly detached return to social themes. During the same year, Coolio's UK and US No. 1 'Gangsta's Paradise' updated the track 'Pastime Paradise' reminding the public of Wonder's ground-breaking work. He capitalized on the renewed attention by recording a collaboration 'How Come How Long' with contemporary producer-performer Babyface.

In 2005, at the age of 55 he released his first new album for 10 years. *A Time 2 Love* was hailed as his strongest in 25 years – a lyrically thoughtful, mature collection of jazz and R&B, which included duets with his daughter Aisha Morris. It returned him to the singles charts with the stomp-funker 'So What The Fuss', and won him his twenty-first Grammy for his vocal performance on 'From The Bottom Of My Heart'.

GENRES

Soul, R&B, Pop, Jazz, Funk

ACTIVE YEARS

1961–present

CLASSIC RECORDINGS

Talking Book, 'Superstition', *Innervisions*, *Fulfillingness' First Finale*, *Songs In The Key Of Life*, *Hotter Than July*

THE YARDBIRDS

VOCAL/INSTRUMENTAL GROUP

The nurtured prowess of successive lead guitarists Eric Clapton (until 1965), Jeff Beck and Jimmy Page helped make The Yardbirds one of the most innovative rock groups of the 1960s. More discreetly influential, however, were more permanent members: Keith Relf (vocals, harmonica), Chris Dreja (rhythm guitar), Paul Samwell-Smith (bass) and Jim McCarty (drums), especially after 1965's 'For Your Love' came close to topping both the British and US charts, and began two years of hits that combined musical adventure and instant familiarity. Highlights included 1965 Top 3 single 'Still I'm Sad', with Gregorian chant overtones, and the Eastern-influenced 'Over Under Sideways Down' from 1966.

In 1966, Samwell-Smith left and Page agreed to play bass until Dreja was able to take over. Beck and Page then functioned as joint lead guitarists until the former's departure in the middle of a harrowing US tour. With an increased stake in The Yardbirds' fortunes, Page suggested the hiring of mainstream pop producer Mickie Most. However, Most struggled to reignite the band's success and The Yardbirds played their final gig in Luton, England in July 1968. McCarty and Dreja reformed the band in the 1990s and they remain a big name in the States. The line-up that cut *Live At B.B. King's* in 2006, with Ben King on lead guitar, appeared in cartoon form on TV's *The Simpsons*.

GENRES

Blues Rock, R&B, Psychedelic Rock

ACTIVE YEARS

1963–68, 1992–present

CLASSIC RECORDINGS

'For Your Love', 'Heart Full Of Soul', 'Evil Hearted You', 'Shapes Of Things', *Yardbirds* (a.k.a. *Roger The Engineer*), 'Over Under Sideways Down'

YES

VOCAL/INSTRUMENTAL GROUP

The quintessential progressive rock outfit, Yes were formed in late–1960s London by bassist Chris Squire, singer Jon Anderson and drummer Bill Bruford. Early albums *Yes* (1969) and *Time And A Word* (1970) only hinted at their potential. *The Yes Album* (1970) featured new guitarist Steve Howe and established them as a major force with virtuoso musicianship, epic songs and Anderson's unique voice and lyrics. The classic line–up was completed when keyboard maestro Rick Wakeman joined for *Fragile* (1971). The 1972 album *Close To The Edge* saw Yes at the peak of their powers.

Alan White replaced Bruford on *Tales From Topographic Oceans* (1973), a double set containing four side-long compositions. Disillusioned by the band's direction, Wakeman left to be replaced by Patrick Moraz on *Relayer* (1974). He returned for 1977's *Going For The One*. Personnel changes continued to bedevil Yes throughout the 1980s and 1990s, with super–producer Trevor Horn drafted in as singer for 1980's suitably titled *Drama*. However, the ultimate schism occurred in 2008 when Anderson, recently hospitalized, was replaced by Benoit David, former singer with a Yes tribute band. Rick Wakeman's son Oliver was also confirmed as an official member, suggesting that it would be business as usual whatever the personnel.

GENRES

Progressive Rock

ACTIVE YEARS

1968–present

CLASSIC RECORDINGS

The Yes Album, Fragile, Close To The Edge, Tales From Topographic Oceans, Going For The One, Tormato, 90125

NEIL YOUNG
GUITAR, SINGER/SONGWRITER

Neil Young was born in Toronto. A highly respected musician, his career has combined facets of acoustic singer–songwriter (as perfected on 1972's *Harvest*) and electric rock'n'roller (1979's *Rust Never Sleeps*). He's also collaborated on and off with Crosby, Stills & Nash and is known as much for his distinctive guitar work as his high, keening tenor voice.

Young first came to prominence in 1967 as a member of Buffalo Springfield, which first united him with Steve Stills. Young's solo career began in 1969 with *Neil Young*. For his next album, *Everybody Knows This Is Nowhere* (1969), he recruited Danny Whitten (guitar), Billy Talbot (bass) and Ralph Molina (drums), collectively known as Crazy Horse. Shortly afterwards, Young joined Crosby, Stills & Nash for an album and tour.

INSPIRATIONAL EVENTS

Events and tragedies that have touched his life have inspired Young's most memorable songs: 'Ohio', about the killing of four students at Kent State University, was written recorded and released by CSN&Y within weeks of the 1970 incident. Closer to home, 'Tonight's The Night' and 'The Needle And The Damage Done' catalogued the human cost of drugs, as paid by friends and colleagues, while the communication problems of his handicapped son Ben was the inspiration behind the 1982 album *Trans*, which saw him experiment with computers and vocoders. A dozen years later Young was moved by Kurt Cobain quoting his 'better to burn out than fade away' lyric in his suicide note to pen him a song, 'Sleeps With Angels'.

The 1970s was Young's most fruitful decade, and one that saw his style and popularity rollercoaster. His country–tinged 'solo' album *Harvest* (1972) was a huge seller, but darkness engulfed Young's work following the sacking and subsequent death by overdose of Whitten, as reflected in *Time Fades Away* (1973), *On The Beach* (1974) and *Tonight's The Night* (1975, recorded in 1973). His next album *Zuma* (1975) featured one of his most celebrated songs, 'Cortez The Killer'.

Young has directed five films under his pseudonym Bernard Shakey, releasing them through his own Shakey Pictures imprint. The second of these was 1979's *Rust Never Sleeps*, a live companion to the album of the same name, which represented a positive reaction to punk from an artist who has never allowed himself to become complacent.

A MUSICAL STATEMENT

Often autobiographical in his writing, Young can also be cynical as in 'Rockin' In The Free World' (1989), a dig at capitalism that was taken at face value by some. The 2006 album *Living With War* was his reaction to the Bush administration's foreign policy and featured a 100-voice choir. The grand gesture, however controversial, was still very much on Young's agenda. While he is a long-time resident of California, it should be noted he retains Canadian citizenship and in 2009 he was made an Officer of the Order of Canada.

Young survived a brain aneurysm in 2005, and the experience inspired the album *Prairie Wind* (2005). Due to the disability of Ben and one of his other sons, Zeke, he has helped found The Bridge School for children with severe verbal and physical disabilities and organizes an all-star benefit concert for the establishment. He has been inducted into the Rock And Roll Hall Of Fame twice: first as a solo artist in 1995, and secondly as a member of Buffalo Springfield in 1997. He has been nominated for multiple Grammy Awards, but to date has won just one.

GENRES

Folk Rock, Hard Rock, Country Rock

ACTIVE YEARS

1960–present

CLASSIC RECORDINGS

Everybody Knows This Is Nowhere, *After The Gold Rush*, *Harvest*, 'Heart Of Gold', 'Cortez The Killer', *Rust Never Sleeps*, *Harvest Moon*

FRANK ZAPPA

GUITAR, VOCALS

In 1964, Frank Zappa formed The Mothers Of Invention. Their albums resembled pop–Dada aural junk–sculptures made from an eclectic heap that, laced with outright craziness, included 1950s pop, jazz, schmaltz and the pioneering tonalities of Stravinsky, Varese and Webern. However, Zappa's intense concern over social issues was never so stifled by burlesque that it could not be taken seriously. *We're Only In It For The Money* (1968) was a chart entry but, too clever for Joe Average, the now greatly augmented Mothers were disbanded in 1969 by Zappa, who then issued *Hot Rats* (1969), a demonstration of his guitar–playing.

Later projects drifted towards lavatorial humour, albeit supported by often beautiful melodies. Yet, in the decade before his death in 1993, Zappa went some way towards establishing himself as a 'serious' composer in the same league as Varese and other of his boyhood idols. He also dabbled as a professional politician, most palpably when the Czech government appointed Zappa its official Trade and Culture Emissary in 1990. Son Dweezil has inherited not only some of his father's talent but also his offbeat sense of humour, and often plays concerts of Zappa senior's music, hoping to bring it to a new generation of listeners.

GENRES

Rock, Jazz, Classical, Avant-garde

ACTIVE YEARS

1965–93

CLASSIC RECORDINGS

We're Only In It For The Money, *Hot Rats*, *Apostrophe (')*, *One Size Fits All*, *Zoot Allures*, *Sheik Yerbouti*, 'Valley Girl'

ZZ TOP

VOCAL/INSTRUMENTAL GROUP

A visually distinctive Texan rock trio comprising Billy Gibbons (vocals, guitar), Dusty Hill (bass, vocals) and Frank Beard (drums, ironically the only non-bearded member), ZZ Top honed their Southern boogie through constant gigging. Gibbons was briefly a protégé of Jimi Hendrix while a member of The Moving Sidewalks.

Supporting The Rolling Stones brought ZZ Top to a wider audience and third album *Tres Hombres* (1973) was the band's commercial breakthrough along with its rootsy hit single 'La Grange'. The 1976 Worldwide Texas Tour saw them take buffalos, cattle and even snakes on the road with them. They went on to experience million-selling success with 1983's *Eliminator* and the singles 'Gimme All Your Lovin'', 'Sharp Dressed Man' and 'Legs'. The music acquired 1980s production values and leant on rhythm machines and synthesizers, while the video clips combined their wacky image with glamorous ladies and hot-rod cars. The MTV generation adopted them as the acceptable face of 'dad-rock' and they were happy to cash in. ZZ Top were inducted into the Rock And Roll Hall Of Fame in 2004 by Keith Richards. They remained alive and gigging in 2010, four decades after their inception, having returned to the rootsier, pre-1980s approach they were most comfortable with all along.

GENRES

Blues Rock, Hard Rock, Boogie Rock, Southern Rock

ACTIVE YEARS

1969–present

CLASSIC RECORDINGS

Tres Hombres, 'Cheap Sunglasses', *Eliminator*, 'Gimme All Your Lovin'', 'Sharp Dressed Man', 'Legs', *Afterburner*

ACKNOWLEDGEMENTS

AUTHOR BIOGRAPHIES

Michael Heatley (General Editor)

Michael Heatley edited the acclaimed *History of Rock* partwork (1981–84). He is the author of over 50 music biographies, ranging from Bon Jovi to Rolf Harris as well as books on sport and TV. He has penned liner notes to more than 100 CD reissues, and written for magazines including *Music Week*, *Billboard*, *Goldmine*, *Radio Times* and *The Mail on Sunday* colour supplement.

Ed Potton (Foreword)

Ed Potton works as the rock & pop editor of *The Times*, and writes regularly on music and film for the paper. He is the co-author of *The Billboard Illustrated Encyclopedia of Music* and *Into the Woods: the Definitive Story of the Blair Witch Project*. Ed has also worked as a producer for Channel 4 television and lectured on music and film at the University of Bournemouth and the Chelsea College of Art. He loves Stevie Wonder and Naomi Watts, and lives in north London.

Richard Buskin (Author)

Richard Buskin is the *New York Times* best-selling author of more than a dozen books on subjects ranging from record production, The Beatles and Sheryl Crow to Princess Diana, Phyllis Diller and Marilyn Monroe. His articles have appeared in newspapers such as the *New York Post*, *The Sydney Morning Herald*, *The Observer* and *The Independent*, and he also writes features and reviews for music magazines around the world. A native of London, England, he lives in Chicago.

Alan Clayson (Author)

Musician and composer Alan Clayson has written over 30 books on musical subjects. These include the best-sellers *Backbeat: Stuart Sutcliffe – The Lost Beatle* (subject of a major film), *The Yardbirds* and *The Beatles* boxes. Moreover, as well as leading the legendary Clayson and The Argonauts, who reformed recently, his solo stage act also defies succinct description. For further information, please investigate www.alanclayson.com.

Joe Cushley (Author)

Joe Cushley has written extensively for *Mojo*, *Q* and *Uncut* and contributed to several books on music, including *The Rough Guide To The Beatles* and *The Mojo Collection*. He compiles albums for Union Square Music, including the acclaimed *Balling The Jack*, *Beyond Mississippi* and *Definitive Story of CBGB* collections. He is a respected DJ and presents a regular show on London's Resonance FM. Joe is currently Theatre and Books Editor of *What's On In London* magazine.

Rusty Cutchin (Author)

Rusty Cutchin has been a musician, recording engineer, producer, and journalist for over 25 years. He began his career in New York as editor of *Cashbox*, the music-business trade magazine. Cutchin has been technical editor of *Guitar One* magazine, associate editor of *Electronic Musician* magazine, and editor in chief of *Home Recording Magazine*. As a recording engineer he has worked on records by artists such as Mariah Carey, Richie Sambora, Yoko Ono, C&C Music Factory and Queen Latifah. Most recently he has been a consulting editor and contributor to several books on home recording, guitar and music history.

Hugh Fielder (Author)

Hugh Fielder can remember the 1960s even though he was there. He can remember the 1970s and 1980s because he was at *Sounds* magazine (RIP) and the 1990s because he was editor of Tower Records' *TOP* magazine. He has shared a spliff with Bob Marley, a glass of wine with David Gilmour, a pint with Robert Plant, a cup of tea with Keith Richards and a frosty stare with Axl Rose. He has watched Mike Oldfield strip naked in front of him and Bobby Womack fall asleep while he was interviewing him.

Mike Gent (Author)

Nurturing an obsession with pop music which dates back to first hearing Slade's 'Gudbuy T'Jane' in 1972, Mike Gent remains fixated, despite failing to master any musical instrument, with the possible exception of the recorder. A freelance writer since 2001, he has contributed to *Writers' Forum*, *Book and Magazine Collector*, *Record Buyer*, *When Saturday Comes*, *Inside David Bowie and the Spiders* (DVD), *The Beatles 1962–1970* (DVD), Green Umbrella's *Decades* and *The Little Book of the World Cup*. Fascinated by the decade that gave the world glam, prog and punk rock, he is working on a novel set in the Seventies.

Jake Kennedy (Author)

Jake Kennedy is a music journalist from west London. He worked at *Record Collector* for seven years, where he was reviews editor. He is the author of *Joy Division & The Making Of Unknown Pleasures*. He writes for numerous magazines and fanzines, and has been a correspondent for Radio 1, BBC 6 and *NME*. He has contributed to Colin Larkin's *Encyclopedia of Popular Music* and the *1001 Albums You Must Hear Before You Die* volume. He is married but never wants kids.

Colin Salter (Author)

Since he bought his first single – 'Reach Out I'll Be There' by The Four Tops in 1966 – Colin Salter has spent a life in music as a composer, performer, promoter and researcher. His first performance, as panto dame singing ABBA and Supertramp

hits in 1975, was succeeded by stints in a Glasgow punk band, a Humberside jazz-folk group and a Kendal jam collective. He worked in theatre for 15 years as a sound engineer and writer of ambient soundtracks. Since 2003 he has been developing a live-music network in rural Cumbria. He moonlights as a golden-oldies mobile DJ.

Ian Shirley (Author)

Ian Shirley lived and pogoed his way through British punk rock and has been buying records and watching bands ever since. He is an experienced music journalist whose feature work and reviews appear in respected magazines like *Record Collector* and *Mojo*. He has written the biographies of Bauhaus, and The Residents as well as two science-fiction novels. He has also written the definitive tome on the links between comics and music: *Can Rock And Roll Save The World?*. He is currently the editor of *Record Collector*'s *Rare Record Price Guide* and has a collection of over 2,000 vinyl albums and 5,000 CDs.

John Tobler (Author)

John Tobler has been writing about popular music since the late 1960s, during which time he has written books on ABBA, The Beach Boys, The Beatles, Elton John, Elvis Presley, Cliff Richard and several generic titles. He has written for numerous magazines including *ZigZag*, *Billboard*, *Music Week*, *Melody Maker*, *NME*, *Sounds*, *Country Music People* and *Folk Roots*. He has written literally thousands of sleeve notes.

PICTURE CREDITS

FURTHER READING

Billboard Guide to American Rock and Roll, Billboard Books, New York, 1997

Bogdanov, V. (ed.), *All Music Guide to the Blues: The Definitive Guide to the Blues*, Backbeat, London, 2003

Bogdanov, V. (ed.), et al, *All Music Guide to Rock*, Backbeat, London, 2002

Brend, M., *American Troubadors: Groundbreaking Singer-Songwriters of the 60s*, Backbeat Books, San Francisco, 2001

Buskin, R., *Inside Tracks: A First-Hand History of Popular Music from the World's Greatest Record Producers and Engineers*, Avon, 1999

Carr, R. and Farren, M., *Elvis: The Complete Illustrated Record*, Eel Pie, London, 1982

Christe, I., *The Sound of the Beast: The Complete Headbanging History of Heavy Metal*, William Morrow, New York, 2003

Cohn, N., *Awopbopaloobopalopbamboom: The Golden Age of Rock*, Grove Press, New York, 2003

Cole, R. and Trubo, R., *Stairway to Heaven: Led Zeppelin Uncensored*, HarperEntertainment, New York, 2000

Draper, J., *Led Zeppelin Revealed*, Flame Tree Publishing, London, 2008

Draper, J., *The Rolling Stones Revealed*, Flame Tree Publishing, London, 2007

Du Noyer, P. (ed.), *The Illustrated Encyclopedia of Music*, Flame Tree Publishing, London, 2003

Ellinham, M., *The Rough Guide to Rock*, Rough Guides, London, 1996

Escott, C. and Hawkins, M., *Good Rockin' Tonight: Sun Records and the Birth of Rock 'n' Roll*, St. Martin's Press, New York, 1992

Fielder, H., *The Beatles Revealed*, Flame Tree Publishing, London, 2010

Fong-Torres, B., *The Hits Just Keep On Coming: The History of Top 40 Radio*, Backbeat Books, San Francisco, 2001

Franklin, A. and Ritz, D., *Aretha: From These Roots*, Villard Books, New York, 1998

George–Warren, H. et al, *The Rolling Stone Encyclopedia of Rock & Roll*, Fireside, New York, 2001

Graff, G. and Durchholz, D., *MusicHound Rock: The Essential Album Guide*, Gale, 1998

Gray, M., *Song and Dance Man III: The Art of Bob Dylan*, Continuum International Publishing Group, New York, 1999

Harrison, H., *Kurt Cobain, Beyond Nirvana: The Legacy of Kurt Cobain*, The Archives Press, 1994

Heatley, M. (ed.), *Rock & Pop: The Complete Story*, Flame Tree Publishing, London, 2006

Hildebrand, L., *Stars of Soul, Rhythm and Blues: Top Recording Artists and Show Stopping Performers, from Memphis and Motown to Now*, Billboard Books, New York, 1994

Ingham, C., *The Book Of Metal*, Carlton Books, London, 2002

Jeffries, N. (ed.), *The "Kerrang!" Direktory of Heavy Metal: The Indispensable Guide to Rock Warriors and Headbangin' Heroes*, Virgin Books, London, 1993

Kent, M., *The Who Revealed*, Flame Tree Publishing, London, 2010

Kozinn, A., *The Beatles*, Phaidon, London, 1995

Larkin, C., *Encyclopedia of Popular Music*, Virgin Publishing, London, 2002

Larkin, C., *The Guinness Who's Who of Sixties Music*, Guinness Publishing, London, 1992

Larkin, C., *The Virgin Encyclopedia of Heavy Rock*, Virgin Books, London, 1999

Larkin, C., *The Virgin Illustrated Encyclopedia of Rock*, Virgin Books, London, 1999

Lewisohn, M., *The Complete Beatles Chronicle*, Harmony Books, New York, 1992

Logan, N. and Woffinden, B. (eds.), *The Illustrated New Musical Express Encyclopedia of Rock*, Hamlyn, London, 1976

Mandel, H. (ed.) *The Illustrated Encyclopedia of Jazz & Blues*, Flame Tree Publishing, London, 2005

McNeil, L. and McGain, G. (eds.), *Please Kill Me: The Uncensored Oral History of Punk*, Penguin USA, New York, 1997

McStravick, S. and Roos, J., (eds.), *Blues-rock Explosion: From The Allman Brothers To The Yardbirds*, Old Goat Publishing, California, 2002

Nathan, D., *Soulful Divas*, Billboard Books, New York, 1999

Pascall, J., *The Golden Years of Rock & Roll*, Phoebus Publishing, New York, 1974

Ritz, D., *Divided Soul: The Life of Marvin Gaye*, Da Capo Press, Maryland, 1991

Salewicz, C. and Boot, A., *Bob Marley: Songs Of Freedom*, Bloomsbury, London, 1995

Shapiro, P., *The Rough Guide to Soul Music*, Rough Guides, London, 2000

Shirley, I., *Pink Floyd Revealed*, Flame Tree Publishing, London, 2009

Slutsky, A., *Standing in the Shadows of Motown*, Hal Leonard Corporation, 1991

Smith, J., *Off the Record: An Oral History of Popular Music*, Warner Books, 1988

Spicer, A., *The Rough Guide to Rock (100 Essential CDs)*, Rough Guides, London, 1999

Strong, M.C., *The Great Rock Discography*, Canongate Publications, Edinburgh, 2002

Thompson, D., *Pop*, Collectors Guide Publishing, 2000

Ward, G., *The Rough Guide To The Blues*, Rough Guides, London, 2000

Whitburn, J., *Billboard Top 1000 Singles 1955–2000*, Hal Leonard Publishing, Milwaukee, 2001

White, C., *The Life and Times of Little Richard*, Harmony Books, 1984

Wyman, B., *Bill Wyman's Blues Odyssey: A Journey To Music's Heart And Soul*, Dorling Kindersley, London, 2001

INDEX

Page references in **bold** indicate major articles, those in *italics* indicate illustrations. Hyphenated page references take no account of intervening illustrations.

ABBA **26–9**, *27*, *29*
Abrahams, Mick 176
AC/DC **30–1**, *31*
Aerosmith **32–3**, *33*
Albarn, Damon 66
Allen, Rick 106
Allman, Duane 34–6
Allman, Gregg 34
Allman Brothers Band, The **34–7**, *35*, *37*
alternative rock music 94–5, 132–3, 234–5, 268, 272, 310–13, 320
Anderson, Ian 176
Anderson, Jon 336
Andersson, Benny 26–8
Animals, The **38–9**, *39*, 160
Areas, Jose 'Chepito' 286
Armstrong, Billy Joe 154
art rock music 284–5, 318
Arthurs, Paul 'Bonehead' 234
Atkins, Chet 110, 254

Bacharach, Burt 98, 136
Baez, Joan 118
Baker, Ginger 100
Baldry, John 178, 304
Band, The **40–1**, *41*, 118
Band of Gypsies, The 162–4
Banks, Tony 146–8
Barber, Chris 224
Barrett, Aston 212
Barrett, Carlton 212
Barrett, Syd 242–6
Beach Boys, The **42–7**, *43*, *45*, *47*
Beatles, The 38, 42–6, **48–53**, *49*, *51*, *53*, 58, 64, 82, 98, 192, 200–2, 228, 234, 276–80, 324
Beck, Jeff 88, 162, 168, 190, 232, 304, 308, 314, 320, 334
Bee Gees, The **54–5**, *55*
Berry, Chuck **56–61**, *57*, *59*, *61*, 118, 158, 280, 306
Best, Pete 48–50

Betts, Dickey 34
Beyoncé 308
Big Bopper, The 166
Big Brother & The Holding Company 182
Black, Bill 252–4
Black Sabbath **62–5**, *63*, *65*
Blind Faith 88, 100
bluegrass music 252
Bluesbreakers, The 88, 128
Blues Incorporated 226, 278
blues music 34–8, 48, 56–60, 84, 88, 116, 134–8, 150–2, 160, 176, 224–5, 268, 278–82
blues-rock music 32–8, 62–4, 88, 100, 128–30, 160–4, 182, 190–4, 206, 278–82, 334, 344
Blur **66–7**, *67*
Bolan, Mark 306
Bonham, John 190, 194
Bon Jovi **68–9**, *69*
Bon Jovi, Jon 68
Bono 310–12
boogie rock music 302, 344
Booker T & The MGs 304
Bowie, David **70–5**, *71*, *73*, *75*, 264–6
britpop music 66, 234
Brodsky String Quartet, The 98
Brown, David 286
Brown, James **76–81**, *77*, *79*, *81*, 202, 212, 236
Bruce, Jack 100
Bruford, Bill 148, 336
Buckingham, Lindsey 128–30
Bunker, Clive 176
Burdon, Eric 38, 248
Butler, Terence 'Geezer' 62, 64
Byrds, The **82–3**, *83*, 104, 118, 122

Campbell, Viv 106
Carter, June 84
Carter Family, The 84
Cash, Johnny **84–5**, *85*, 298

Celtic music 224
Chandler, Chris 38
Channing, Chad 228
Charles, Ray 328
Cher 36
Chic 72, 264
Chicago blues music 168, 226
Chicago (group) **86–7**, *87*
Chimes, Terry 90–2
Christian, Charlie 60, 184
Clapton, Eric 34, 40, **88–9**, *89*, 100, 101, 128, 162, 186, 212, 226, 314, 334
Clark, Gene 82
Clarke, Michael 82
Clash, The **90–3**, *91*, *93*, 108, 212
classical music 138, 264
Clifford, Doug 102
Clinton, George 78–80, 236
Cobain, Kurt 228–32, 338
Coldplay **94–5**, *95*
Collen, Phil 106
Collins, Allen 206
Collins, Judy 118
Collins, Phil 28, 146–8, 194
Coltrane, John 286
Cook, Stuart 102
Cooke, Sam **96–7**, *97*, 160, 202
Cool, Tre 154
Copeland, Stewart 248–50
Cornick, Glenn 176
Costello, Elvis **98–9**, *99*, 166
country and western music 48
country music 56, 84, 116–20, 158, 196–8, 204
country rock music 40, 82, 118, 122, 338–40
Coverdale, David 194
Cox, Billy 162, 164
Cream 88, **100–1**, *101*, 168, 190
Creedence Clearwater Revival **102–3**, *103*
Crickets, The 166
Crosby, Bing 72

Crosby, Dave 82, 104
Crosby, Stills & Nash **104–5**, *105*, 338
Crudup, Arthur 'Big Boy' 252

Daltrey, Roger 322–6
dance music 172–4, 210, 214
Davis, Dave 188
Davis, Miles 286
Davis, Ray 188
Dawson, Colin 322
Deacon, John 262–6
Dee, Kiki 180
Deep Purple 64
Def Leppard **106–7**, *107*
Delaney & Bonnie 88
Densmore, John 112–14
Derek & The Dominoes 34, 88
Detours, The 322
Di Anno, Paul 170
Dickinson, Bruce 170
Diddley, Bo **108–9**, *109*, 226
Dion, Celine 180
Dire Straits **110–11**, *111*
Dirnt, Mike 154
disco music 26–8, 54, 304
Dixon, Willie 56, 168, 190
Domino, Fats 200
Donegan, Lonnie 48, 224
Doors, The **112–15**, *113*, *115*, 168
doo-wop music 76, 140–4
Dreja, Chris 334
Dylan, Bob 40, 82, 96, 110, **116–21**, *117*, *119*, *121*, 162, 166, 202, 230, 240, 276, 296, 300, 320

Eagles, The **122–5**, *123*, *125*
electric blues music 168, 226
electronic music 210, 242, 268
Eminem **126–7**, *127*
Eno, Brian 72–4, 284, 310–2
Entwistle, John 322, 326
Epstein, Brian 50–2, 278
Ertegun, Ahmet 194

E Street Band, The **296–301**, *297*
Everly Brothers, The 200
experimental rock music 268, 318

Faces, The 304
Fairport Convention 220
Fällskog, Agnetha 26–8
Felder, Don 122–4
Ferry, Bryan 284
Fleetwood, Mick 128–30
Fleetwood Mac **128–31**, *129*, *131*
Flying Burrito Brothers, The 122
Fogerty, John 102
Fogerty, Tom 102
folk music 84, 116–20, 150–2, 300
folk rock music 40, 82, 104, 116–20,
    124, 176, 190–4, 290, 300, 340
Foo Fighters, The **132–3**, *133*, 232
Franklin, Aretha **134–9**, *135*, *137*, *139*
Franklin, Carolyn 134–6
Free, The 212, 266
Frey, Glenn 122
Funkadelic 78, 236
funk music 76–80, 140–4, 236, 258–60,
    272, 286–8, 294, 328–32

Gabriel, Peter 146–8
Gale, John 318
Gallagher, Liam 234
Gallagher, Noel 234
Garcia, Jerry 150–2
Garfunkel, Art 290
Gaye, Marvin **140–5**, *141*, *143*, *145*
Geldof, Bob 246
Genesis **146–9**, *147*, *149*
Gentle Giant, The 146–8
Gibb, Barry 54
Gibb, Maurice 54
Gibb, Robin 54
Gibbons, Billy 344
Gilmour, David 232, 242–6
glam rock music 26–8, 68–74, 178–80,
    262–6, 284, 306
gospel music 76, 84, 96, 116–20,
    134–8, 184, 200–4
Grateful Dead, The **150–3**, *151*, *153*
Green, Peter 128–30
Green Day **154–5**, *155*
Grohl, Dave 132, 230–2
grunge music 230, 274
Guns N'Roses **156–7**, *157*, 266

Guthrie, Woody 298
Guy, Buddy 186

Hackett, Steve 146–8
Haley, Bill **158–9**, *159*
Hammett, Kirk 218, 288
Hammond, John, Jr 160
hard rock music 30–2, 68, 88, 100,
    106, 112–14, 156, 160–4, 170, 182,
    190–4, 206, 262–6, 302, 314–16,
    322–6, 338–40, 344
Harris, Emmylou 110
Harrison, George 48–52, 240
Hawkins, Ronnie 40, 118
Hayward, Justin 222
Headon, Topper 90, 92
Heartbreakers, The 240
heavy metal music 30–2, 62–4, 106,
    156, 218, 314–16
Hendrix, Jimi **160–5**, *161*, *163*, *165*,
    202, 228, 344
Henley, Don 122–4
Herman's Hermits 118
Hetfield, James 218
High Numbers, The 322–4
Hill, Dusty 344
Hillman, Chris 82
hip-hop music 80, 126, 236, 286–8
Hollies, The 104, 118
Holly, Buddy 108, 160, **166–7**, *167*
Hooker, John Lee 116, 288
House, Son 320
Howlin' Wolf 160, **168–9**, *169*

Iggy Pop 72–4
indie music 66, 94
Iron Maiden **170–1**, *171*

Jackson, Michael 144, **172–5**, *173*,
    175, 314
Jagger, Mick 74, 204, 212, 278–82
James Gang, The 124
jam music 34–6
Jardine, Al 42–4
jazz fusion music 34–6
jazz music 134–8, 150–52, 224,
    248–50, 258, 272, 286, 328–32
jazz rock music 286–8
JBs, The 76–80
Jefferson Airplane 182
Jethro Tull **176–7**, *177*

Jimi Hendrix Experience, The 160–4
Johansen, Jai Johanny 'Jaimoe' 34
John, Elton 136, **178–81**, *179*, *181*,
    200, 266
Johnson, Johnnie 56, 58
Johnson, Robert 100, 160
Johnston, Bruce 44, 46
Jones, Brian 278–80
Jones, Mick 90–2
Joplin, Janis **182–3**, *183*
Journey 32, 286
Judas Priest 64

Kath, Terry 86
Kiedis, Anthony 272
King, B.B. 88, 160, **184–7**, *185*, *187*
Kinks, The **188–9**, *189*, 324
Knopfler, David 110
Knopfler, Mark 110, 308
Kool & The Gang 80
Korner, Alexis 226, 278
Krieger, Robbie 112–14

Laine, Denny 222
Latin rock music 286–8
Leadon, Bernie 122–4
Led Zeppelin 64, **190–5**, *191*, *193*,
    195, 320
Lennon, John 48–52, 60, 72, 136,
    166, 280
Lewis, Jerry Lee **196–9**, *197*, *199*, 204
Little Richard 160, **200–5**, *201*, *203*, *205*
Lodge, John 222
Love, Courtney 230
Love, Mike 42–6
Lydon, John 'Johnny Rotten' 290
Lyngstad, Frida 26–8
Lynyrd Skynyrd 36, **206–7**, *207*

Madonna **208–11**, *209*, *211*
Mann, Manfred 118
Manzanera, Phil 284
Manzarek, Ray 112–14
Marley, Bob 88, **212–17**, *213*, *215*,
    217, 330
Martin, Chris 94
Mason, Nick 242–6
Mauldin, Joe B. 166
May, Brian 232, 262, 266
Mayall, John 88, 128, 130
Mayfield, Curtis 136, 140, 160

McCartney, Paul 48–52, 136, 166,
    202, 222, 280
McGuinn, Roger 82
McIntosh, Peter 'Tosh' 212–14
McKay, Andy 284
McKernan, Ron 'Pigpen' 150–2
McVie, Christine 'Perfect' 128–30
McVie, John 128–30
Melsner, Randy 122–4
Memphis blues music 184–6
Mercury, Freddie 262–6
Metallica 64, **218–19**, *219*, 266, 288
metal music 190–4
Michael, George 136, 266
Miles, Buddy 162–4, 286
Miracles, The 140, **276–7**, *277*, 328
Mitchell, Joni **220–1**, *221*
Mitchell, Mitch 160, 164
Molina, Ralph 338
Moody Blues, The **222–3**, *223*
Moon, Keith 322–6
Moore, Warren 276
Morris, Aisha 330–2
Morrison, Jim 112–4
Morrison, Sterling 318
Morrison, Van **224–5**, *225*
Mothers of Invention, The 342
Mott the Hoople 72
Muddy Waters 56, 160, **226–7**, *227*

Nash, Graham 104
Navarro, Dave 272
New Animals, The 38, 248
new country music 206
Newsted, Jason 218
new wave music 98, 248–50, 284
Nicks, Stevie 128–30
Nirvana 132, **228–33**, *229*, *231*, *233*,
    238, 274
Novoselic, Chris 228, 232

Oakley, Berry 34–6
Oasis 66, **234–5**, *235*
Orbison, Roy 240, 296
Osbourne, John 'Ozzy' 62–4

Page, Jimmy 190, 194, 314, 334
Paltrow, Gwyneth 94
Parfitt, Rick 302
Parliament–Funkadelic **236–7**, *237*
Parliaments, The 236

Parsons, Gram 82
Parton, Dolly 54
Patton, Charley 168
Paul Butterfield Blues Band, The 118
Pearl Jam 238–9, *239*
Perry, Joe 32
Peter, Paul & Mary 116
Petty, Tom 240–1, *241*
Pinder, Mike 222
Pink Floyd 242–7, *243, 245, 247*
Plant, Robert 190–4
Plastic Ono Band 60
Pogues, The 92
Police, The 38, 212, 248–51, *249, 251*
pop music 26–8, 56, 96, 134–8, 154,
    172–4, 178–80, 188, 196, 202,
    258–66, 286–8, 296–300, 304,
    310–14, 322–6, 328–32
pop rock music 106, 320
post-grunge music 132
Presley, Elvis 76, 158, 196–8, 204, 212,
    252–7, *253, 255, 257*
Presley, Priscilla 254–6
Preston, Billy 202
Price, Alan 38
Primal Scream 236
Prince 258–61, *259, 261*, 288
progressive rock music 176, 222,
    242–6, 262–6
psychedelic music 150–2, 210,
    294, 302
psychedelic rock music 38–46, 82,
    88, 100, 112–14, 160–4, 182, 236,
    242–6, 302, 334
pub rock music 98
punk blues music 320
punk music 90, 198
punk rock music 154, 230, 270–2, 290

Queen 72, 262–7, *263, 265, 267*

Radiohead 268–9, *269*
Ramone, Dee Dee 270
Ramone, Tommy 270
Ramones, The 270–1, *271*
rap music 32, 126, 272
rap rock music 272
R&B music 38, 56, 76–80, 96,
    134–44, 160, 172–4, 184–6,
    200–4, 224–6, 242, 258–60,
    276–82, 324, 328–32, 334

Redding, Noel 160, 164
Redding, Otis 34, 136, 202
Red Hot Chili Peppers, The
    272–3, *273*
Reed, Lou 72, 318
reggae music 212–16, 248–50
Relf, Keith 334
R.E.M. 274–5, *275*
Richards, Keith 60, 278–82
Robertson, Robbie 40
Robinson, Smokey 276–7, *277*
rockabilly music 84, 130, 158, 166,
    196–8, 252–6, 264
rock music 68–74, 90, 110, 134–8,
    150–2, 172–4, 188, 202, 248–50,
    258–60, 270, 278–82, 294–300,
    304, 310–12, 322–6, 328–32
rock'n'roll music 30, 38–40, 56–60,
    84, 102, 158, 166, 196, 200–4,
    252–6, 278–84, 296
rock pop music 128–30
Rogers, Bobby 276
Rollie, Gregg 286
Rolling Stones, The 36–8, 58, 122,
    140, 166–8, 204, 226, 278–83,
    279, 281, 283, 330, 344
Ronson, Mick 70–2
Rose, Axl 156
Ross, Diana 54, 142
Rossi, Francis 302
Rossington, Gary 206
Roth, Dave Lee 314–16
Rotten, Johnny 290
Roxy Music 222, 284–5, *285*, 318
Rutherford, Mike 146, 158

Samwell–Smith, Paul 334
Santana 128, 286–9, *287, 289*
Santana, Carlos 286–8
Savage, Rick 106
Scott, Bon 30
Seeger, Pete 298
Sex Pistols, The 90, 290–1, *291*
Shrieve, Michael 286
Simon, Paul 166, 292
Simon & Garfunkel 292–3, *293*
Simonon, Paul 90–2
skiffle music 48
Slash's Snakepit 156
Slovak, Hillel 272
Sly & The Family Stone 294–5, *295*

Small Faces 304
soft rock music 54, 86, 178–80, 290
Sonny & Cher 118
soul blues music 184–6
soul music 70–80, 134–44, 160,
    172–4, 200–4, 224, 236, 276,
    294, 328–32
Soul Stirrers, The 96
southern rock music 34–6, 102,
    206, 344
Spector, Phil 296
Spencer, Jeremy 128
Springsteen, Bruce 200, 212, 240,
    296–301, *297, 299, 301*
Squire, Chris 336
Starr, Ringo 48–52, 306
Status Quo 302–3, *303*
Steel, John 38
Stewart, Rod 96, 304–5, *305*
Stills, Steve 104, 338
Sting 248–50
Stipe, Michael 274
Stone, Sly 294
Strummer, Joe 90–2, 108
Summers, Andy 38, 248–50
surf music 42–6
Sutcliffe, Stuart 48–50
Swaggart, Jimmy 196
swamp rock music 102
swing music 172–4
symphonic rock music 222

Taupin, Bernie 178–80
Taylor, Mick 280–2
Taylor, Roger 262, 266
The Edge (guitarist) 310
Thomas, Ray 222
Thompson, Paul 284
thrash metal music 218
Took, Steve 306
Townshend, Pete 162, 322–6
T. Rex 306–7, *307*
Trucks, Butch 34
Tucker, Maureen 318
Turner, Ike 160, 308
Turner, Tina 160, 308–9, *309*
Tyler, Steven 32

U2 310–13, *311, 313*
Ulrich, Lars 218
Ulvaeus, Björn 26–8

Valentine, Hilton 38
Van Halen 314–17, *315, 317*
Van Halen, Eddie 232, 314–16
Van Zandt, Steve 296–8
Van Zant, Ronnie 206
Vaughan, Stevie Ray 72
Vedder, Eddie 238
Velvet Underground, The 112,
    318–19, *319*
Vicious, Sid 290

Wailers, The 212–14
Wakeman, Oliver 336
Wakeman, Rick 336
Walker, T-Bone 60, 160, 184
Ward, Bill 62–4
Warhol, Andy 318
Warwick, Clint 222
Waters, Roger 242–6
Watts, Charlie 278
White, Meg 320
White, Ronnie 276, 328
White Stripes, The 320–1, *321*
Who, The 92, 108, 122, 322–7,
    323, 325, 327
Williamson, Sonny Boy 168, 184
Wilson, Brian 42–6
Wilson, Carl 42–6
Wilson, Dennis 42–6
Wings 52, 222
Winwood, Steve 88, 100
Wonder, Stevie 140–2, 328–33,
    329, 331, 333
Wood, Ron 282, 304
Wright, Richard 242–6
Wyman, Bill 278, 282

Yardbirds, The 88, 190, 334–5, *335*
Yes 222, 336–7, *337*
Yorke, Thom 268
Young, Angus 30
Young, Malcolm 30
Young, Neil 338–41, *339, 341*

Zappa, Frank 342–3, *343*
ZZ Top 344–5, *345*